# PANDIT JAWAHARLAL NEHRU AND THE PEASANTRY (1920-1947)

# PANDIT JAWAHARLAL NEHRU AND THE PEASANTRY (1920-1947)

Dr. Ravindra Kumar

ATLANTIC PUBLISHERS & DISTRIBUTORS

*Published by*
**ATLANTIC PUBLISHERS AND DISTRIBUTORS**
B-2, Vishal Enclave, New Delhi - 27
Phone: 5413460

*Sales office*
4215/1, Ansari Road, Darya Ganj
New Delhi - 110002
Phone : 3273880



*Typeset at*
APD Computer Graphics
B-2, Vishal Enclave, N. Delhi - 27

*Printed in India at*
Mehra Offset Press
New Delhi

# Foreword

I feel immense pleasure in penning the foreward to "Pt. Nehru and the Peasantry" the young and renowned scholar, Dr. Ravindra Kumar's research work on Pt. Jawahar Lal Nehru, celebrated leader of common masses and the builder of modern India. Pt. Nehru, a great visionary of this century, had started his public life in the midst of the farming community of Oudh in 1920 and had organised the farmers to free themselves of the bonds of exploitation thrust on them by the landlords, Zamindars and Talukdars and, above all, by an alien rule. He forced the government into enacting laws for the betterment of the farmers. The unity of the farmers of Outh permeated a wave of awakening among the farmers of the country which injected a new strength into the movement for the achievement of independence. The farming community shook off its age-old slumber and came to the fore-front to break the fetters of slavery.

Nehru many a time led the farmer's movement and played a significant role in strengthening their bodies at the local, provincial and national levels resulting into the liberation of farmers from the bondage of Zamindars and others exploitations and the farmers emerged a strong force in the overall progress of the nation after the achievement of independence. Panditji knew that farmer is the builder of this country and agriculture is the fountain-head of the national progress. He, therefore, worked for the advancement of this sector and left no stone unturned in its overall improvement and introduction of new and modern farming techniques. He had, way back in 1963, pointed out, "I may emphasise over the establishment of heavy industries and steel plants; I may talk of technical and scientific advancement as also progress in other sectors; but what is of paramount importance is agriculture and its advancement. Only self-reliance and the advancement of the farmers can decide the destiny of the nation."

This research work based on an uphill task accomplished by Nehru before and after the independence for the farming community and their future achievements shall be very beneficial to the general public, political scientists, historians and those interested in the welfare of the farming community and shall prove as a milestone on the subject. I congratulate the research scholar for his endeavours in shaping this enterprising work.

Rajesh Pilot
Minister of State for Surface
Transport, Govt. of India

# Preface

Agriculture plays the foremost role in the Indian economy and 76 per cent of its population is directly involved in agriculture for its livelihood. This 76 per cent population, the farmers, has been the bread-winners of this country. And now they have made the country self-dependent in food, smashing all the records of food-production which is a matter of great pride not only for the country but for the farming community itself. The cardinal group of the country, the farmers, have led a life of humility, subjugation and exploitation and have borne the cruelties perpetrated by the Talukdars, landlords and moneylenders, but all these cruelties helped them in glorifying their personality. In the long run came a time for the redemption of respect and glory of the farmers. This is a long story and in the length and breadth of this story it would be doing injustice to the farming community on the one hand showing dishonesty to the coming generations and on the other if we disassociate Pt. Nehru from this story who acted as a beacon light to the farmers in liberating them from the cruelties, by helping them lead a self respecting life and by inspiring by making them self-reliant and inspiring them build a glorious future after shaking off the fetters of slavery and for inculcating in them a philosophy of truth, non-violence and fearlessness. Dishonesty in the sense that the coming generations shall be deprived of those thoughts of Nehru which he held and put into action for the unchecked progress of the farmers.

The future generations should not be deprived (even unintentionally) of the most significant political chronology which revealed Nehru to establish a strong link between the movement for the achievement of independence and the farming community as a result of which the rural masses of the nation came into the forefront to help unfetter the country from the chains of slavery. Keeping these two facts into view, I had decided to do research work entitled "Pandit Nehru and the Peasantry". Pandit Nehru possessed a multi-dimensional personality and the farming community was an essential part of his personality, the significance of which can never be underestimated. Therefore, inspired by the fact lost the most significant aspect of Pandit Nehru's towering personality, his philosophy and thinking on the farming community should remain untouched, I started work on this line and the final result of my humble efforts is before the readers.

Words fail me in expressing my thanks and gratitude to Shri Rajesh Pilot, ex-Minister of State for Surface Transport, Government of India and Shri Hitendra Desai the former Chief Minister of Gujarat for their help in the completion of this work. I express my heartfelt gratitude to institutions like National Archives, New Delhi; State Archives, Lucknow; Nehru Memorial Museum and Library, New Delhi; National Gandhi Museum and Library for their active help in procuring the original manuscripts and other literature on the subject. I cannot forget the valuable co-operation extended to me by Dr. Hari Dev Sharma, Shri Lakhmendra Khurana, Dr. (Mrs.) Malti Malik and Prof. K.L. Malik during the completion of this project.

In the end, humbly bowing to the farming community, the representative of a strong majority of our community, I dedicate this book to the political scientists, historians, the common people, especially to the farmers with the hope that they will constantly carry the nation forward on to the path of progress according to the ideals of Pt. Nehru because this was prime message and chief mission of his life for which he lived.

RAVINDRA KUMAR

# Contents

# CHAPTER I

## Relations with the Oudh Peasantry (1920-21) Results of the relations: An analysis

Beginning of Pt. Jawahar Lal Nehru's service to the peasants and well-shaped thinking outlined for their future, marks in the early period of 1920, before the non-cooperation and Khilafat movement, with the contact of the peasants of Oudh. "On June 6, 1920, two hundred and ten peasants from Pratapgarh district, having assembled from distant rural areas, under the leadership of Shri Ramachandra marched 50 miles to tell their tale of woes, sufferings and exploitation to the chief leaders."[1] These peasants, bearing clear marks on their faces of landlords' debt and other cruelties and exploitation, reached Allahabad to show the real condition of the peasant-class.

At Allahabad on the bank of river Yamuna, they camped and Nehru, along with other local leaders, came to see them. They came out unreservedly before Nehru with inhuman treatment and exploitation meted out to them by landlords and made it clear, "These adverse circumstances caused by these landlords, are now intolerable."[2] Therefore, they appealed Nehru and his co-workers "They should return with them to rural areas and witness themselves the circumstances and come to their rescue."[3] Thus, these peasants, with their utmost humility, requested Pt. Nehru and his fellows and they agreed to return home having been assured that they would witness themselves the conditions in the villages.

Nehru was so much impressed that without least care of scorching heat, he got ready to do his best in their interest; though a few days earlier in the midst of May he came leaving his mother Smt. Swarupa Rani and his beloved wife Kamala Nehru at Mussorrie. As the promise his was, Nehru, with his colleagues, rushed to the village of district Pratapgarh and there he observed the plight of the peasants. He reached the distant villages which were not linked with railway stations and roads either."[4] Having a complete survey of the peasants condition Nehru underwent a revolutionary change which occurred in two forms. Firstly, in the words of Prof. V.K.R.V. Rao, "Nehru could have his contact with the masses through these peasants and thus, young Nehru, educated at Harrow and Cambridge, observed in the Western Culture, now turned towards the peasant class. He sat beside them, dined with them and engrossed in their problems and hardships. He chanced to have a talk directly with the peasants and held their meetings and realized that "these people live on the mercy."[5]

During his stay among these peasants Nehru saw the soul of India and a new thinking took place about the future of India and it was secondary radical change in his being. Nehru has put himself this unique experience with the contact of peasants, "To me the departure (in the villages of Pratapgarh) was divine voice. We found there the entire rural area was at fire of excitement and people were in the grip of religious ignorance.'[6] Nehru took this contact with peasants most significant and fortunate for his future career.

He accepted the fact that the peasant class had been illuminated afresh and was on the way to collective deliverence. And such a powerful illumination! which, in later years, enlightened his thinking and guided him to a proper direction. If Nehru could not have his contact with peasants? to quote Nehru, " I am struck with wonder to think this that if I had not been at Allahabad (when the peasants of distt. Pratapgarh marched to Allahabad) what would happen then? I had plenty of time at that time, I was not busy elsewhere. My contact with peasants, later or sooner, was quite possible but very manner in which I went with them, it would certainly be different and the impression I received, would certainly have been otherwise."

## Effects of Nehru's Contact with Peasant-class

Nehru's contact with peasants of Pratapgarh in Oudh brought out so many important facts which showed clearly exploitation of this class; some of them can be summed up as follows :

*(i) Face to Face of Peasant's Economy.*

First and foremost effect of Nehru's contact was that he understood the economic condition of the peasant class. He witnessed their sufferings, oppressions, imposed illegal tax, disowning from land and houses, cruel beatings and every sort of cruelty done to them by both representatives of landlords and police. Not only this but also an eye was kept on them what they produced after long day toil and in the end everything was seized and they were left to starve. There was a group of men who had no land since their land was confiscated by imposing excess tax upon them. These people wandered homeless. Here the land was good but it was meant for the landlords, the farmers were levied more heavily than the land itself and as a result the peasants has no economic ground. A good number of families lived on a small patch of land. The landlord took undue advantages of this state of helplessness of these peasants and compelled them to pay tax, though it was illegal. Enough strange it was ! that it was the bare reality of the whole of Oudh, Allahabad, Faizabad, Pratapgarh, Rai Bareily where Jawahar Lal Nehru raised the curtain through his metticulus survey to expose the real picture.

"The peasant class had no choice but to bear cruelty and starvation. That is why they borrowed a little money or grain just to have a square meal and the landlords charged as much interest as they desired and if they failed to pay money with interest, they were disowned in no time."[7] Peasant's economic condition which was good-for-nothing, was now quite clear to Nehru. He was sure about peasant's condition all over the country. To quote him, "Indeed, the life of peasant is troublous and miserable. It is shameful that the peasant who feeds the whole world, has no guarantee for his three months' bread. The landlords and moneylenders took away all their crops for their debts and interest. The manner in which the landlords harness the farmers like an ass, is a blot in the fair name of humanity."[8]

It is necessary to make it clear here that the picture which

Nehru had about the peasants' condition made him conclude that "the method of landlords and the condition of peasant-class in relation to land is ancient and traditional and its poverty had never ceased. The method which has been divised to crush villages is equally based on the economic condition of district in Oudh."[9] Thus, Nehru's contact with the peasants brought him face to face to peasant's economy. Taking it as basis he had drawn a clear picture of peasant's plight whether it was the question of his nude poverty or his conservatism or his slavery. For example, he had taken it for granted that "the peasant class, with no economic existence; and without bread and shelter, leads a worse life than a bandit labourer. He is never allowed to have a seat before the landlord or moneylender, but contrary to this his life depends on his mercy. He cannot be treated as human-being but he is constantly being pushed away into sordid conditions of life and not to say that economic condition is the sole factor behind the phenomenon."[10]

## Clarity of Future-Plans

Nehru's contact with the peasants of Pratapgarh made him clear that entrance in rural areas is an imperative need of today instead of urban politics. The existence of the country lies in villages and the thinking of the welfare of these down-trodden people could be meaningful and relevant for the future of the country. In fact, the peasant-class looked up to Nehru and his co-workers with hope and aspiration. It not only shocked him but also made him ashamed and he was taken aback how the majority of the people of India, living a life of exploitation and poverty had been neglected so far."[11]

With the strong feeling of repentence and remorse he decided the direction of his work. For first three days he stayed with the peasants of Pratapgarh; afterwards he continued to be with peasants not only of Allahabd or Pratapgarh but also of the whole Oudh. The organization of the peasants of Oudh became his mission and he came out with flying colours in his mission. He linked the peasant-class with the freedom movement and measured British slavery and peasant's economy with the same scale. This was the reason that during non-co-operation and Khilafat movement, the peasants of Oudh and United Provinces, at the call of Nehru, responded with a vengeance, for the sake of their existence and stood up against the exploiters both native and alien. As a result, the peasants, during the non-co-operation movement, did the charismatic deeds which were applauded by the Russian historians, "the movement (Non-co-operation and Khilafat) in the autumn of 1920 spread for and wide in rural areas and the peasants' struggle in Oudh reached its climax; although the effects of Congress and Khilafat movement were limited yet the organized national movement and the peasants' movement were linked together itself."[12]

## Life-long Relationship with the Peasants

Nehru's contact with the peasants of Oudh established his life-long relationship with them. On the one hand, Nehru had unwavering faith in them, and he could develop an inner relationship with them on the other and became one with them. An example illustrating his devotion – "Nehru would go to the peasants in a car and stayed with them at their huts, they, in response, repaired the tracks through which Nehru had to pass. Nehru was obliged to address the peasants' meeting far and wide, hundreds of peasants, without caring of weather, came out perspiring to repair the roads, if needed, they would rebuilt it."

*Example of Nehru's harmony with them* – As he saw the peasants work hard on the way, he walked on foot for miles, leaving his car aside. In this way he could bring together police and C.I.D. officers who were accompanying him and thus resisted posse for a long time which had come to crush them.

Were dog-tired but obliged to go with them. It was the result of Nehru's complete identification with the peasants that in 1930 at the time of civil disobedience, he said addressing the peasants of Oudh : "My life is meaningless until I help the peasants to get rid of their grievances; and freedom of the country has got no meaning so long as the peasant is burning in the flames of exploitation."

He was so cautious and serious about the interest of the peasant-class he visited repeatedly the places where people were stricken with awe and terror due to the ill-treatment of landlords and police and the incidents of disowning of peasants frequently took place, so that the peasants might sighed a breath of relief.

Simultaneously, "He set his mind on the rescue of peasants' physical torture and other illegal troubles caused by the agents of landlords. Nehru got information in no time of such incidents and he tried his best to look into the matter."[14] It certainly restricted the activities of the landlords. Owing to it Nehru's seriousness towards the peasants, the landlords felt a bit embarrassed, "they were frightened and began to think about their safety and the state government had to make a promise to bring an amendment bill."[15] In 1936 Sardar Patel remarked commending highly this great service, in the peasants' meeting in U.P., "In the absence of Nehru this meeting is like a ship without sailor. He is fully aware of their grievances, sad plight and troubles. The service rendered by him and his wife (Mrs. Kamala Nehru) stands still unparalleled. He, for the sake of the peasants, abandoned his aristocratic living and both have neglected everything as personal life and family. How can we step ahead without Nehru who is gloomy at heart for our sorrow and whose heart had sunk at our poverty and who had become a beggar leaving his prosperity aside? How can we put even a single step without Nehru, a man of helping nature? In spite of his absence, his blessings shower upon us. We pray to Almighty to help us to move on the way shown by him and again pray that as a sailor he should cast anchor to save our sinking ship."[16]

## Clarity of Landlord's Policies

Nehru's contact with the peasants of Oudh brought out to Nehru the policies and acts of landlords. He studied the tradition and system of landlordship and after complete analysis an understanding was developed that the peasants must get rid of this system. Although this understanding will be discussed in ensuing pages with complete details yet briefly we can say, "Nehru was firmly of the opinion about the term landlordship that this word is a deceptive word, literally it signifies that all the landlords possess a great area of land." He arrived at right conclusion that one hundred and fifty years long British administration is a great support to this system. The landlord-class has ever been enjoying unrestricted privileges and the peasant-class has been reduced to miserable condition which cannot be put in words. The British Government neither pays attention to this nor draws the attention of the landlords though it talks about the safety of the rights of landlords. The opinion of Nehru came into light that, "the landlord-class feels pride in imitating the British officers and on the other hand they do not miss any chance to inflict cruelty upon the peasants to save their existence. The British officers are on the side in this cruelty since their well-being, lies in the existence of these landlords."

## Beginning of Nehru's systematic social life

Even before the contact with the peasants of Oudh in 1920 Nehru was highly interested in social work and as the Secretary of Allahabad Congress Committee he keenly took interest in the peasant-class but in the real sense his systematic social life began with the contact of the peasant of Oudh. He has acknowledged himself that "the peasants have taught me to speak among the people without hesitation. Before that I could hardly speak before the people."[17] Here an important change in Nehru's life is marked which took shape later on. Secondly it became memorable incident in Nehru's life because in the province for the first time in the history of struggle for freedom, the peasant-class as an organization, entered into politics and it was not supported by contemporary veteran leaders of Indian Congress."[18] It was an imitable instance for others with the beginning of Nehru's social life.

## Step Towards Peasant's Guidance

After his contact with the peasants Nehru was confronted with many social evils and problems in various fields of the peasant-class. Nehru was determined to deal with these evils with iron hands and he had been striving all his life to put them to an end but having toiled with them he concluded, "Though the peasants of Faizabad and Rai Bareily joined non-co-operation, with all their demands, at the call of Gandhiji and after the incidents of the first struggle for freedom in 1957, it stood up against unlawful taxes and cruelties of the landlords but unfortunately at several places the peasants resorted to violence. For the first time, the peasant-class showed collective strength on a large scale in political freedom but the condition of Gandhi's non-violence was thrown to the winds."[19]

Having seen this, Nehru planned in such a way so that the peasants might keep violence at an arm's length and struggle with the power of soul. It did not matter whether he agreed with Gandhiji or not regarding the peasants' struggle but it was sure that non-violent peasants' struggle became his mission and he guided it successfully. He had judged it that "the experiment of non-violence on a mass scale cannot be taken merely a dream because Gandhi's way of non-violence at Champaran in Bihar and at Kaira in Gujarat partly paved the way for success and comparatively proved better. He thought over the matter deeply that people's approval for violence all the time was entirely wrong and now non-violence could not be separated from the fact. The peasants would have to acquire a great strength through non-violent means and it would be the real strength of the people for the great cause of the country.

Thus, it would not be irrelevant to say that Nehru was inspired to decide the line of action for future just after his contact with the peasants of Oudh following the path of non-violence. The significance of his contact which began in 1920 at some villages of distt. Pratapgarh and later on spread in the whole area of Oudh, Faizabad, Rai Bareily and Lucknow, cannot be underrated."[20]

Nehru's this contact was of vital importance and a unique incident for the interests of the peasants and future struggle for the cause. Consequently, its effect was observed later in non-cooperation and Khilafat movement which started in 1920. In United Provincies the peasants' class gave an impetus force and undoubtedly it was the leadership of Nehru. It is also the fact that "the impression of country-wide non-cooperation movement under the leadership of Gandhiji and Congress, linked with Khilafat movement cannot be denied, but in the rural areas of United Provinces especially in Oudh (Eastern U.P.) the basis of people's strength was the peasant-class which was organized by young Nehru and his friends."[21]

The condition of the peasants which Nehru witnessed going from village to village, made him realize the real sorrows of the people for which, later on, Nehru tried his best before independence and even after independence whether he took the step for land reforms or to end the landlordism or to make the peasants self-reliant by improving agricultural device. As stated earlier, the peasants contact made Nehru clear as what to do about the future of the peasants who represent the majority and his contact with them continued throughout his life.

## References

1. Home Political 1920 (June), 6/20. N.A.I. New Delhi.
2. *Ibid.*
3. *Ibid.*
4. Home Political 1920, 7/20. National Archives of India, New Delhi.
5. Rao, V.K.R.V., The Nehru Legacy, New Delhi, 1970, p. 5.
6. "That visit a revelation to me. We found the whole countryside afire with enthusiasm and full of a strange excitement. Enormous gathering would take place at the briefest notice by word of mouth. One village would communicate with another and the second with the third, and so on, and presently whole villages would empty out and all over the field there would be men and women and children on the march to the meeting place or more swiftly still, the cry of Sita Ram-Sita. Ra-a-a-am would fill the air, and ravel for in all directions and be echoed back from other villages, and then people would come – streaming out or even running as fast as they could. They were in miserable rags, men and women, but their faces were full of excitement and their eyes glistened and seemed to expect strange happenings which would, as if by a miracie, put an end to their long misery." – Nehru, Pt. Jawahar Lal, An Autobiography.
7. Kumar, Dr. Ravindra, Sardar Vallabhbhai Patel and Com. Mao Tse Tung: A Comparative Study, Muzaffarnagar, 1988, p. 22.
8. *Ibid.*, pp. 23-24.
9. Home Political 1921, F. No. 7/21. N.A.I., New Delhi.
10. Kumar, Dr. Ravindra, Sardar Vallabhbhai Patel and Com. Mao Tse-Tung: A Comparative Study, p. 25.
11. "They showered their effection on us and looked on us with loving and hopeful eyes, as if we were the bearers of good tidings the guides who were to lead there to the promised land. Leo King at them and their misery and over-flowing gratitude. I was filled with shame and sorrow. Shame at my own easy going and comfortable life and over petty politics of city which ignored this vast multitude of semi-naked sons and daughters of India, sorrow at the degradation and overwhelming poverty of India. A new picture of India seemed to rise before me, naked, starving, crushed and utterly miserable. And their faith in us, casual visitors from the distant city, embarrassed me and filled me with a new responsibility that frightened me." – Nehru, Pandit Jawahar Lal, An Autobiography.
12. "The non-co-operation movement of the winter of 1920 was visible clearly in rural areas. Peasant's upheaval got its greatest effect in United Provinces and especially its east distt. (Oudh) in the year of 1921-22 where the reminiscences of 1857-59 were still fresh. Peasant's discontentment had begun at Faizabad and Rai Bareily where the farmers who mainly

belonged to the lower class, laid hand on the landlords, destroyed their crops and damaged their houses. In small towns, traders and money-lenders were assailed. Their leaders started coming out from the peasants; some of them utilized the small plays stayed in the fair held at rural areas, poets and musicians, going from pillar to post, prepared people for the great cause. Under the leadership of Pt. Nehru the peasants of the province happened to be into an organic whole known as 'Eka' in 1921-22. Here the revolutionary peasants strengthened the Khilafat movement and this was what Nehru dreamt of. It is to be discussed in succeeding pages in detail. Though there was no outline for action clearly chalked out, but due to his active selfless harmonizing strenuous efforts, peasants' upheaval proved effective against the feudal lords and money-lenders. During the struggle, the seeds of peasants organization appeared sprouting at some places. Due to his active participation in the peasants revolt, for the first-time, young Nehru who encouraged other Congress members to work for the peasants organization, was arrested. The effect of Congress and Khilafat movement was limited yet both were inseparably linked together. The appeal of these rebel peasants made Gandhiji realize the condition of the peasant class. The peasants' movement of United Provinces left clearly a good impression and marked the beginning of a new era in the History." – Antonova, B.L. and others, History of India, Moscow, U.S.S.R. 1982, pp. 557-8.

13. Home Political, 1930, F. No. 257/x/30. N.A.I., New Delhi.
14. Home Political 1930, F. No. 257/30, N.A.I. New Delhi.
15. Home Political 1921, F. No. 13/21. N.A.I., New Delhi.
16. Parikh Narhari and Shah Uttam Chand, Speeches of Sardar Vallabhbhai Patel, Navjivan, Ahmedabad 1950, p. 304.
17. "These peasants took away the shyness from me and taught me to speak in public. Till then I hardly spoke at a public gathering; I was frightened at the prospect, especially if the speaking was to be done in Hindustani as it almost always was. But I could not possibly avoid addressing these peasants gatherings, and how could I be shy of these poor unspohisticated people? I did not know the arts of oratory and so I spoke to them, man to man, and told them what I had in my mind and in my heart. Whether the gathering constituted of a few persons or of ten thousand or more I stuck to my conversational and rather personal method of speaking, and I found that, whatever might be lacking in it. I could at last go on. I was fluent enough. Perhaps many of them, could not understand a great deal of what I said. My language or my thought was not simple enough for them. Many did not hear me when the gathering was very large for my voice did not carry far. But all this did not matter much to them when one they had given their confidence and faith to a person." Nehru, Pt. Jawahar Lal, An Autobiography.
18. Namboodiripad, E.M.S., A history of Indian freedom struggle, Trivandrum 1988, p. 382.
19. *Ibid.*
20. *Ibid.*
21. *Ibid.*

# CHAPTER II

# Nehru and the Problem of the Farming Community

**(a) Nehru's Conception of Farmers' Problem**
**(b) Ideals born out of it : growth of socialism**

The problem of peasant-class was an integral part of Nehru's social and political thinking since he new it very well that at the root of these problems lies the crude role of landlords and the selfishness of the British Government. Nehru was much worried at the sad plight of the peasants when he stepped into his social life and presided over the Congress Conference in 1929; It made him aware of the peasants' condition prevailing all over the country because "the money-lenders inflicted cruelties upon them and landlords and traders were also equally callous to them."[1]

Having a comprehensive view over these problems which were haunting Nehru's being all the time, he presented his stand or the ideal of socialism as a remedy for the crisis but before probing into deep of the aspect; it is essential to know the exact problems of the peasant-class of that time because the peasant class had been suffering under the yoke of money-lenders' encumbrance and the British Empire brought about but a dramatic change in it. The result of this change was, "it enslaved social and economic life and it resulted that the middle and upper-middle class, having given up self-respectable occupations, served as the link between the people and the Britishers. This middle class was to satisfy the belly of the Britishers and itself as well."[2]

During the year of 1910-12 the report of a distt. in Western India makes clear the condition of the peasant class throughout the country. The peasants all over the country became prey to famine and other natural and human calamity." Class of Punjab, U.P. Central India, Western and Middle Gujarat, Karnataka and Maharashtra is same still today as it was. According to the report of this area, "the total population, in accordance with census of the year of 1901 was 6,30,672 and 3,85,194 people's profession was farming and 1,24,937 men and 51,008 women were helpers, 5484 men were blacksmiths or carpenters, 7597 khati and 38354 were harijans and all these men helped the peasants in some or the other way and depended entirely on farming. Only 9454 were traders and money-lenders who were the bankers of the rural people and lent them money."[3] The year of 1909-10, according to land-arrangement, worth-cultivating land was 9,63,664 acre and thus the peasants owned about 8 acre land per man. About one-third of the land was barren, and if it rained heavily, the crop would be possible, so famine continued due to which the peasant class and its helpers went on getting poorer."[4]

"The Govt. during the year of 1900-10 gave debt of Rs. 68,004 to six and half lac people within ten years (which falls as some pies to the share of an individual)[5] ; rest of the debt which was necessary to suffice the bare necessities of the peasants, was to be borrowed from moneylenders or landlords and this was the peasants' helplessness to which they had no alternative. Eventually, they had to give up their lands. Nehru studied seriously these reports and came upon the problems.

### Illiteracy-conservatism

The first and foremost problem behind the miserable condition of the peasant-class was illiteracy and conservatism. The Indian peasants had been not only illiterate for centuries but also they were disorganized and conservative. The traders charged prices of commodities as they pleased and the peasants had to pay interest on the debt as much as the former wished. "The rate of interest was Rs. 6 per month that is Rs. 72 per year. This was too much for the peasants to pay. Roughly, it was an anna per ruppe for a month. Besides, interest on interest was charged and this was the open exploitation of these helpless peasants."[6] Cursing their fate, the peasants tolerated all this; as Nehru himself has put, "the peasants muttered in fear, Ram, Sita Ram....." Briefly, the peasant was born in debt and died in debt and handed over this inheritance to coming generation.

Since the Govt. was imperialist and it needed badly these mediators – feudals, landlords and money-lenders for its economic advantage so it could not object to this exploitation and undue advantage of the illiteracy of these peasants. "It supported these exploiters. There was no question to sympathise with them. The real condition was that even a peon of Govt. came and treated harshly these illiterate and superstitious peasants and not only this but showered abuses over and humiliated them......."[7]

## The Problem of Zamindar's Exercise of Power and Peasant-class

Illiteracy and conservatism were the important factors of peasants' exploitation on the one hand, zamindar's exercise of power used against them was another on the other hand. To quote Nehru, "Zamindari system used lathi, guns and police to inflict maximum cruelties upon the peasant class and having filed false suit against them, disowned them and even sent them into prison."[8] It was the crude reality. The report of C.I.D. of Indian Govt. makes it clear, which was prepared with the help of the statement of the secretary of Congress Committee of Gorakhpur distt. published in 'Pratap'. It was published on May 31, 1931 and it reported, "The Congressmen or their colleagues (peasants) were thrashed severely by Zamindars; they were made stand in the blazing sun and after five minutes they were flayed off. That is – if the peasant is under any circumstances, zamindar, without least hesitation, used utmost power against them and it was a serious problem and there was no way to escape this cruelty. The support of the British Govt. to the Zamindar class made it more fatal; both followed the policy of maintaining their existence at the cost of the peasants ever caring for the interests of each other. The Zamindar class which had been on the mercy of kings and princes for centuries, ruled over the peasant class with all their excesses.

## Problem of Disorganization of Peasant-class

Disorganization of this class was another problem which existed for a long time. Due to this, the peasant class became the victim of exploitation and slavery; and the upper class was having undue advantage of this weakness. Its result was that whenever some peasants dared speak or stood against this exploitation, they had to lay down their life. Not only this if some peasant group raised voice against, it was put down strictly too. But the peasant class, surprising enough, never took a lesson and it fell prey to disorganization. This was the reason that Nehru expressed his great anxiety over the problem in 1929 and said addressing the peasants of Allahabad, "At least ten thousands volunteers must come forward among you."[10] He again said in no uncertain terms, "If the peasants are united, this regime of lathi cannot go for a long time."[11]

## Other Problems

The peasants were in the grip of other problems as drinking, drugs-addiction, gambling and mutual prejudices and enmity. All these vices made them weak in social, economic and political field.

## Nehru's views and their implications over problems

Nehru took peasant problem as the National problem because such a vast agricultural country was represented by these peasants and it was not good to take their problems at local or provincial level. On November 17, 1936, this national problem, he put before the huge crowd of 1,50,000 people and said, "The real condition of India can be seen through the grovelling poverty of common people and the Congress will only be able to hit this national problem if peasants' organization co-operates in full measure. Not only this but also the present system is to be changed into a welfare socialist pattern and this socialism cannot be achieved so long as the British Govt. exists here."[12] Therefore, the peasants, along with their workers, will have to achieve freedom and only then they will be able to show their real existence. For this great task, Nehru gave top priority to their organization. At some place in Madras province, he said in this reference, "All down-trodden will have to struggle unitedly on a large scale to get rid of their troubles. In the western province, the peasants showed their power and naturally it resulted in expected advantage."[13] This is the only way to struggle unitedly for the peasants of the whole country. He again stressed, "Once if you are united, your are all powerful. You must learn this. If you want to end your troubles, be fearless, since if you are not fearless, zamindars or their agents or policemen will surely frighten you."[14] Nehru referred the example of the power of unity of Bihar and United Provinces."[15] In this way, Nehru was trying continuously to link the peasants with the main current of the country, by inspiring and revolutionizing them and it was his great achievement. In 1930 under the Presidentship of Nehru, the working committee of Indian Congress passed a resolution entitled 'Congress' Resolution on "Peasants Programme" in which all sorts of security, help, development and co-operation was assured.

## Immediate Solution

Nehru put forward some immediate and practical devices before the peasants to solve their problems, along with their organization.

(i) *Regarding Taxation*

As it has been discussed in preceding pages, the landlords, deceiving the peasants due to their illiteracy and conservatism, received the land-tax without any receipt. As a result, the peasants had to pay land-tax again in the lack of proof. This problem was in the practice in Orissa and Barar and in some parts of Punjab and Bihar besides eastern province. So on March 20, 1931, at the national level, he said in the meeting of peasants : "Many a time, the tenants were asked to pay 4, 6 or 8 annas per rupee. There should be a clear provision that the landlord must give receipt of land rent or accept it."[16] Nehru asked all Congressmen and the peasants to work for the task; and on this basis on March 22, 1931, the secretary of the Congress Committee wrote to the Congress of Fatehpur that they should not pay any tax without receipt. The peasants did the same ; and the peasants and the landlords were at bitter ties over this issue. Although the Government reports presented the whole affair in different forms, but as is clear in appendix 4, that the peasants refused to pay the tax in the absence of receipt and using force, the landlords were attacked.

(ii) *Regarding Leadership and Organization*

The second immediate solution shows a deep insight of Nehru which he not only suggested about the leadership of the country and the organization but also followed it strictly. It may be possible that the peasants' troubles may end in home-rule or they may get rid of the landlords with the help of true leaders of the country but the Indian Congress should not dream of independence at the cost of peasants because it is the only power which will take us to independence. It is an important aspect of Nehru's understanding in which his socialism was lying.

It is important to know that Nehru never accepted anything at the cost of peasants. When in July 1931, he was invited in the round table conference, Nehru rejected the very formation of the Congress due to having less representation of the peasant class."[17] It would be more important to tell that on July 20, Nehru asked Emerson "to end these big landlords."[18]

For Nehru, the measurement of steps taken for the interest of peasants was never political. For example, Punjab can be taken, in the year of 1934, for the first time in the country. Itahad Party of Punjab passed Karz Mansukhi Law which relieved the farmers of Punjab from the exploitation of landlords. Some leaders gave this law a political colour but Nehru called it socialist step taken towards the interest of the peasants and remarked, "Punjab has paved the way for the rest of the country. This is the innovation in the economic history of India."[19]

### (iii) *Regarding Police*

Undue pressure on the peasants in favour of the landlords was also their problem. Nehru had studied this problem very well and presented his views to hit at the root of the problem. He declared, "if the police inflict cruelty or does excesses, it should be strongly protested."[20] Nehru reiterated that this fearlessness will have to be observed in the organization of peasants. For any reason if they would not show such fearlessness or could not be organized, they must inform at once about the cruelties of the police to the nearest office of the Congress."[21]

Nehru concluded that this problem could easily be controlled. After all, the police is not the servant of the landlords but of the Government and the landlords misuse it. If the peasant-class becomes aware of it, it can be avoided.

(iv) *Regarding Judiciary*

At Lal Ganj in U.P. Nehru said, regarding the suits filed in courts against the peasants, "you should not be afraid of suits filed against you. You should be much determined to face the court. Mind it, if you have the fear of court or prison, neither you will be able to good of yourself nor of the country. Tell the court everything frankly and honestly. You should not be in the grip of fear at that time."[23] The statement of Nehru, regarding the courts, contains the very truth, there is only a single aim behind setting these courts – to demoralise the peasants so that they may astray. Besides, it has got no aim. When the peasant has been physically suffering for centuries, he should not be under the mental strain inflicted upon by the courts."[23]

Thus Nehru understood the problems of the peasants and tried his best to solve them and made it clear that the peasants need badly organizational strength; until they gain it, independence will be a distant dream. In 1930 he sent his message for the peasants of Rai Bareily.

**Nehru on peasants' problem and socialism**

As has been said earlier that Nehru came in public contact through peasants. Although Nehru, during his study at Harrow and Cambridge, came in the contact of the Western socialists yet on returning India, after his contact with the peasants of Oudh, he put forward the idea of ideal socialism which is still relevant in the reference to the peasants.

His idea of taking society on the path of socialism in political and historical fields, is of vital importance. He wanted peasant-class to be self-reliant. In fact, his socialist ideal regarding the peasants is a great achievement as well as contribution to India. To quote Prof. Rao, "In 1927, during his trip of Russia, Nehru's socialism was under the influence of Marxism but it is important to note that he wanted to abolish poverty through awakening of people. He wanted to change their slavery and tendency as well; and he desired to put aside the policy of supremacy, customs and control of a particular class since without this no economic, social or cultural development was possible."[23] Not only this but without this, socialism, the re-making of the peasant-class and the country as well is not possible at all. Thus, Nehru, during the struggle for freedom, studied seriously the problems of the peasant-class and developed socialism which aimed at the welfare of the peasant-class.

After studying completely the problems of these peasants, he formed his opinion on basic economic circumstances – poverty, landlordship, elitism etc. – and he rejected strongly the disparity on the basis of birth nor accepted the caste system."[24] He held in this regard, "The peasants after all area one, their problems are same, the basis of the slavery is same, their weakness (illiteracy and disorganization) is same. Then what is the basis of their disparity? Again, "The reality of India is her poverty and this poverty cannot be diminished until a drastic change is brought about into the very fabric of the structure and it is replaced by equality and prosperity through socialism."[25]

The concept of socialism and its realization through the peasants was quite clear in the mind of Nehru and he was again any sort of exploitation or pressure on people. He wanted that land should be under one who tills it, and not of exploiter or Zamindar. He said, addressing a peasant meeting, "If I am asked, theoretically I can say that I am deadly against the landlord class. I am of the opinion that every one should be the owner of his land. One who tills it, will be its owner of his land. One who tills it, will be its owner. I cannot agree to any other concept. People will have to decide it too. If this idea of mine is acceptable to all, I shall be happy. I have expressed my views unreservedly before you."[26] But Nehru further talked of handing over this basic right to the peasants or it should be earned by the peasants themselves. "But there is a burning question before you (peasant-class) that is you must be well equipped to fight with hope and courage against this present political and economic crisis and after the conquest over it, to establish socialist system, strengthen organizational power."[27] This agreement of Nehru was very significant and it symbolised his political comprehension because the peasant-class which was representing majority and was basic source of production and the very basis of economic system, could play an important role in establishing socialist system and could achieve the status of equality. Nehru expressed his views regarding this in 1930, at Lahore Congress Conference, "I must make it clear that I am a socialist and republican as well and never I have faith in Kings and Princes or the Kings created by modern capitalist system who are supposed to be better than the Kings of ancient times."[28] Socialism means a complete change and it can be brought about by abolishing poverty and disparity but this is not possible only for Indian National Congress. Believing in the very fact, he said to the peasants, "Independence means a comprehension solution of peasants' every problem and this will be achieved in soicalism and if this is not achieved, all is meaningless. The very imagination of socialism is possible only in independence and this will be achieved only with the help of peasants' power. For Nehru, socialism and independence are interested. Once defining independence he said in the meeting of peasants at Allahabd, "The real meaning of independence is to put people's woes and troubles to an end; and the proper system of taxes, right of land and its possession. Such independence would relieve them, and at the same time it means to end alien rule and the end of any sort of Kingship or lordship. Our independence means to establish Panchayati Raj in the country where there will be no difference between the ruler and the ruled and every one will be his own master and share equally national affairs. The Panch who are your temporary rulers, will be your servants. This present system of administration which is based on force and make people obey it by force. The another system of administration is in which people are taken into confidence through Panchayati Raj and no force is used in any walk of life. In this system no use of gun, army or police is needed. This is the ideal system which can help people to get rid of their troubles and other problems; and this is the socialist system."[29] That is Nehru wanted to establish democratic system through Panchayati system because the woes of peasants had made it clear to him that until peasant-class comes out collectively for the sake of their own affairs, neither it will be able to get rid of sorrows nor the country will progress.

### The end of poverty and socialism

To Nehru socialism is a powerful means of abolishing poverty; it matters not if Nehru has taken socialism on global scale, but it is related with common man of India and particularly with the peasant-class, and it aimed at effacing poverty from the face of humanity. So economic freedom has not occupied less importance than political freedom in his thoughts. In the year of 1936, his speech delivered in the Congress Conference at Lucknow which is given in detail in appendix 18, proves this fact : "The solution of the problems of India and the world lies in socialism. This is the best way. Socialism is a social aspect, philosophy of life and thus it impresses me."[30]

Briefly we can say there are three pillars of Nehru's socialism —

(i) To achieve social goal for India ;

(ii) Its achievement with Congress and means for National liberation ;

(iii) Achievement of its Ideal in India's circumstances.

India was under the yoke of slavery and it was essential for all to come forward unitedly to struggle against the British empire so Nehru, with a comprehensive understanding, worked collectively for the freedom and Indian National Congress instilled hope and faith into people though there was not representation of all the sections of society in it. He knew that Indian circumstances were to be probed into for equality and prosperity. His first mission was the freedom of the country because it alone could solve the problems of the peasants; however it might be partly. It was right that after the end of alien rule, many peasants' problems as tax, irrigation, landlords and others, could be solved and the peasants became self-reliant by increasing their production.

After independence of the country, Nehru stepped to establish socialism though it needs not be mentioned here. But to make it clear is essential that there were the problems of the peasants behind all his thinking and for their solution he was always worried. His ideal socialism was exclusively dedicated to the peasants' problem and their progress and he left no stone unturned to do this.

## References

1. During the First World War, when the Great Britain burdened their most of the military expenses upon their colonies, rapid plunder of Indian wealth caused dreadful consequences for the people. As a result of bad economic relations of the world during war, the import of Jute, Cotton and other technical crops affected the interest of the peasants. The landlords and the traders made up their loss through exploitation of producers and peasants. During the years of 1911-27, the debt of money-lenders on

peasants was just double about 600 crore rupees. Owing to the exploitation by landlords, colonial-state and money-lenders, there was a rapid increase in the transfer of land. Most of tne peasants had to be disowned due to pawning or sale of their land.

"Along with peasants, the farmers, artisans, small traders etc. had to face terrible ordeals. Even before and during World War I products of many off-shoots of agriculture-architecture and cottage industries declined, consequently, income of a large number of artisans was adversely affected." Not only this but during the year of 1918-19 and the year of 1920-21, the crops went unexpectedly worse and economic condition of the country became more serious. Due to the lack in food production, people faced famine while the import of grain remained the same and mainly the peasant-class was affected. People were already suffering but 130,0000 people died due to the spread of influenza." – Antonova, K.A. and others, History of India, Moscow, p. 540.

2. Peasants struggle....page 26.
3. *Ibid.*, p. 33.
4. *Ibid.*, p. 34.
5. *Ibid.*, pp. 34-5.
6. "There is no record of insecured debts in the years of 1910-1925; and it was not possible to have such records and the prevalent rate of interest was very high that was an anna per rupee and after six months compound interest was to be charged. This was the debt of money-lenders." – Peasants struggle, p. 35.
7. Kumar, Dr. Ravindra, Sardar Vallabhbhai Patel and Com. Mao Tse-Tung: A Comparative Study, 1988, p. 18.
8. Home Political 1931, F. No. 46 – National Archieves of India, New Delhi.
9. 'Inhuman atrocities on the peasants of Gorakhpur.' "Both the Rabi and Kharif crops of the Gorakhpur district have been damaged owing to floods and drought in the first case and frost and hail in the other. Besides this, barring a few, all the zamindars of this locality realise three-fold, four-fold and five-fold of the stipulated rent. Moreover they extort Bhusa and begar as they choose. The peasants have themselves been ruined this year owing to the condition of the crops and the prevailing prices. Over and above this, the zamindars and their agents are perpetrating such atrocities that a man's heart is rent to behold them. The Zamindars get the kisans recklessly beaten by Lathis. This excess is practised particularly on those who are either supporters of the Congress or its volunteers. The Nadirshahi oppression has grown so much that the public is crying out for deliverance. The Kisans are made to climb trees and are thrown down from there and they are left only when they have become senseless after being thrown down three or four times continuously. They are made to stand in the hot sun of this season for the whole day and are beaten with shoes every five minutes. They are tied with ropes and suspended with head or feet downwards and they are released only when blood begins to ooze out of their mouth and nostrils. Peasants are made to lie in the sun with their breasts or backs loaded with bricks and stone. A number of persons have died up till now as a result of these atrocities and others are

lying on death-bed owing to blows from lathis and sticks and other atrocities. Many atrocities of this sort are practised in broad day-light. Whole villages have been burnt down. In a number of villages the houses of many peasants have been burnt. Women are caught by the hair and dragged and beaten. Some wicked and immoral zamindars and their agents are forcibly violating girls in villages. All these atrocities have been in full swing even after the Gandhi-Irwin pact. The attention of the Government officials of the district was drawn in this direction but they have put wax into their ears. May we hope that the higher government officials will turn their attention this way and will take immediate steps to put a stop of the highhandedness prevailing in Gorakhpur." — Home Political 1931, No. 47/31. N.A.I., New Delhi.

10. Home Political 1931, F. No. 247., National Archives of India, New Delhi.
11. *Ibid.*
12. Home Political 1936, F. No. 37/3, National Archives of India, New Delhi.
13. Home Political 1936, F. No. 39/4, National Archives of India, New Delhi.
14. *Ibid.*
15. "The Zamindari system is so bad that the tenants cannot make any great improvements under that system. I am telling out the great agrarian movement in the United Provinces, the agrarian movement which took place a year before the non-co-operation movement. Thousands of them went to prison. They were perfectly peaceful but still, in order to crush them, these were firing at them on several occasions and thousands went to prison and for the moment they were rather frightened. But still they forced the government by their united action to change the whole tenancy law which effected them.....where agitation was strongest for greater remissions were given where there were little agitation; and in the neighbouring Province of Bihar where there was no agitation among the peasantry there was no remission at all although the tenants were in a very bad way. And when government was asked, Government said: They did not ask for it, why should we give? Once you organise yourself you became strong. Therefore the lesson you should learn is this. If you want to put an end to your troubles you must not be afraid; because if you are afraid of your Zamindar or Zamindar's agent or policemen, then you are done for." — Pt. Jawahar Lal Nehru. Home Department Political 1936, D. No. 38/4., National Archives of India, New Delhi.
16. Home Political 1931, F. No. 24/2. National Archives of India, New Delhi.
17. "I (H.W. Emerson) found the Pandit (Jawahar Lal Nehru) less hostile to the Round Table Conference than I had expected. He disapproved of its composition, because it gave little representation to peasants etc and to the depressed classes." — Home Department Political 1931, F. No. 32/31; National Archives of India, New Delhi.
18. '"The Greater part of our talk (between Emerson and Nehru) was concerned with the United provinces and part that Congress has played during the past four months. He (Nehru) had a great deal to say about the inequities of the landlords, their rack-renting oppression of tenants, and lack of contact with them and interest in them. As mentioned above, he would like to abolish big landlords. He attempted to defend the attitude

Congress had taken since the settlement, but he was more ready to accept facts than Mr. Gandhi.... His general line was that the kisans like any other body of labourers had the right to organise themselves and that in view of their inherent lack of education and experience they naturally turned to Congress for the purpose. Congress, in short, was the labour organisation of the Kisans. He pushed this anology further still and said that just as any other labour organisations were entitled to advice labourers what wages they should accept from their employers so the Congress were entitled to advise the kisans what rents they should pay to the land owner." – Home Department Political 1931, F. No. 32/31; National Archives of India, New Delhi.

19. Peasants struggle........p. 65.
20. Home Political, N.D.O. 3710 (Dated 27.3.31); Provincial Archives Lucknow (U.P.).
21. Home Political 1931, N.D.O. 3710., Provincial Archives, Lucknow (U.P.).
22. *Ibid.*
23. Rao, Shri V.K.R.V., The Nehru Legacy, Bombay, 1971, p. 52.
24. *Ibid.*, pp. 52-3.
25. Home Political 1931, F.No. 33/XI/and K.W., National Archives of India, New Delhi.
26. *Ibid.*
27. *Ibid.*
28. "I must frankly confess that I am a socialist and a republican and not a believer in kings and princes or the order which produces the modern kings of industry who gave greater power over the lives and fortunes of men than even the kings of old, and whose methods are as predatory as those of the old feudal aristocracy. I recognize, however, that it may not be possible for a body contituted as is this National Congress, to adopt a full socialistic programme. But we must realize that the philosophy of socialism has gradually penetrated the entire structure of society the World over almost the only paints in dispute are the pace and method of advance to its full realization. India will have to go that way too if she seeks to end her poverty and inequality, though she may evolve her own methods and adopt the ideal to the genius of the race." Nehru, Pt. J.L., Presidential Speech of Lahore Session of I.N.C. Dec. 1929.
29. Home Department Political 1930, F. No. 33/11 and K.W. National Archieves of India, New Delhi.
30. President's Speech of 49th Session of Indian National Congress, April 1936, Lucknow, published by the Allahabad Law Journal Press, 1936.

# CHAPTER III

# Political Movement, Movement of Peasantry and Nehru

**A. A Study of their relationship**

**B. Establishment of a relationship between the two**

The struggle, which the Indian people did on political level from 1920 to 1942, that cannot anyhow be disassociated from the peasantry. As the philosophy of Mahatma Gandhi's non-violent Satyagraha (truth's persistence) got associated with the Non-cooperation and Swadeshi (native) movement, same way the peasantry with heart and soul busied itself in the country's freedom and it remained in the foremost role of about all the subsequent political movements; and the main contribution has been of Jawaharlal Nehru to establish inner relations between the two. Nehru was of the view that the National independence movement and the peasantry's movement were complementary to each other. Through his intense political thinking he came to the conclusion that economic interest of the peasantry was closely related to the country's political independence; so political independence was the first step on which the peasantry had to proceed. It was the cause that for the sake of independence he delivered message to the peasantry to struggle under the leadership of Mahatma Gandhi and the Indian National Congress. In this context he had said that the Swaraj (self government) was meant the full inclusion of the peasantry's interests and for that we were engaged in political combat. He had said to the country's inhabitants and especially the peasants, "It is never to be forgotten that till full Swaraj (self government) does not come and we do not eradicate miseries-pains of the peasants by that time the Congress and

Mahatma Gandhi cannot sit quietly. For full Swaraj (self government) our effort will be continuing definitely. The Congress has begun combat for the sake of misery-pain of the peasants and the Swaraj (self government). There is no difference between this combat and your struggle. Both are the same."[1]

Not only this but Nehru always increasingly enthused participation of the peasantry in the country's struggle and during Salt Satyagraha when the peasantry gallantly faced cruelty of British regime, Nehru became impatient and he delivered message, "If our strength will grow, we will attain the Swaraj. We will not rest till the miseries of the peasantry will not end. And such time will surely approach."[2]

For the country's independence from 1920 to 1947, three very important political movements, under the leadership of Mahatma Gandhi, were stirred. These were – the Non-cooperation and Swadeshi (native) movement in 1920, Civil disobedience movement or Salt Satyagraha in 1930 and Quit India Movement in 1942; and the peasantry wholeheartedly participated in these three struggles. In this participation there had been the main contribution of Nehru.

### Non-cooperation and Khilafat movement and the peasantry

Through the experience gained from consequences of stirring countrywide political movement against the Rowlat Act of 1919, "Mahatma Gandhiji concluded that to stir Satyagraha movement it was essential to chalk out a detailed and systematic programme, only then the struggle would be kept non-violent."[3] According to his (Gandhiji's) thought the two obviously different stages were essential for the countrywide Non-cooperation movement against the colonial rule. "The first stage included the following forms of boycott directed against the colonial rule – (a) abondoning of conferred posts and honours, (b) boycott of the government functions etc., (c) boycott of elections of the legislative assemblies, (d) boycott of the government schools, colleges and courts, (e) boycott of foreign articles. The second stage was the non-payment of the government taxes."[4]

With the programme's purpose the movement was about to begin on 1st August, 1920, and Gandhiji with colleagues was busy in organising and preparing with the close cooperation of the Khilafat movement's leaders. The Khilafat movement was organised by the Mohammedan intellectuals and religious leaders with the purpose of protecting the rights of Turkey's Sultan – Calif – and that movement had just assumed anti-imperialist character because in the sight of Indian Mohammedans the fall of Usman empire and overthrow of Calif was directly linked in the east with western powers and especially British policy."[5] In India for the bigger part of Mohammedan population the anti-colonial aspect of that movement was more important than its religious aspect. The common activists of that movement often derived only one important meaning of Khilafat as the opposition of the Britishers – movement against them. Due to the freedom war then being fought by Afganistan at the North-Western frontier of India, this tendency became more clear. The rebel Pathan tribal groups of North-Western Frontier Province had actively supported this struggle of the neighbouring Mohammedan country.

Thus, with the Hindu-Muslim cooperation the countrywide Non-cooperation and Khilafat movement was the struggle fought for the first time for the country's independence. In it there had been important role of the peasantry. Before analysing (role) we should also study of that time's peasants movement's circumstances and rising of those.

## Rise of peasants movement

In 1920, the peasantry's resistance rose against the British rule and its Landlord system in about the whole of India and in February-March in the countryside the resistance by the peasantry got strengthened before the beginning of Non-cooperation and Khilafat movement. This resistance was not due to Gandhiji's leadership or the complete inspiration from him though he had already led the peasants struggles of Champaran-Motihari etc. areas of Bihar in 1917 and of Kaira district of Gujrat in 1918. The reason of this resistance was increased by 25 per cent in rent at national level. The basis of this increase were made prior thirty years but before 1920 in thirty years the conditions of peasantry and countryside India had been deteriorating. Having viewed deteriorating conditions of the peasantry, justifiably there should have been done re-assessment through abatement of rent but contrary was done."

Against this injustice of the government there haad been this reaction in the peasantry and as in ref. 12 of the chapter I, it is stated, 'mostly the eastern parts of United Provinces were the places of rising of peasant's commotion where Jawahar Lal Nehru himself had led the peasants'.[7] At the rest of the places either minimum or maximum awakening of the peasants was there and at some places it was even at its extreme. Consequently these spontaneous activities of the peasants, which remained continued by the middle of 1921, were mercilessly repressed by the force of army and police and thousands of people were arrested."[8] Sultanpur district of United Provices was at the top of these peasants activities throughout the country. Spontaneously the peasants were on the path of struggle in Punjab, Gujarat, Kerala and Bengal etc. before the Non-cooperation movement. For example the struggle of Sikh peasants of Punjab against the Mahants who had controlled the income of properties and land holdings of Gurudwaras and increased the rent. Though this movement, by its inherent senses, was positively the struggle of peasants, small arable land owners and tenant farmers against the feudals while its another face was also to reinstate democratic practices in the life of Sikh community. The meaning by it that the Eka agitation in Uttar Pradesh (then United Provinces), Akali peasants struggle in Punjab, Mopla peasants insurrection in Kerala etc. were obvious peasantry's struggles at that time. Only in Gujarat's Kaira Gandhiji had begun with. As the Non-cooperation and Swadeshi movement was begun, at that time the peasantry was not fully connected with this movement but it was most essential to take the men in the street in mainstream of the National movement. And how this whole task could have been possible without participation of the peasantry because it represented from 70 to 80 per cent people. But it is historical fact that the peasantry on large scale was taken in the mainstream of the National independence's movement. Its struggles were linked with the movement and at that time United Provinces remained in the foremost role of this task behind which the main inspiring source was Jawaharlal Nehru.

In United Provinces the peasantry's agitation got linked with the Non-cooperation and Swadeshi and Khilafat movement and it provided this movement with enough strength and it is true, as it is also already mentioned, 'though there was very limited influence of the Non-cooperation and Khilafat movement in the villages but due to the peasants movement being linked with this, it gained momentum fully in the countryside. The peasantry became participant in the movement continuing under the leadership of Mahatma Gandhi."[9] Not only this, the Congress party got strengthened. For example data published in *Young India* in 1921 can be cited .....

"Swaraj fund 4,10,737. It was an integral part of the Non-cooperation movement,

The Congress Party's membership rose to 3,28,966.

Charkha spinners numbered 2,81,525

Legal practice was ceased 113

Terminated Panchayats numbered 3,000

National schools numbered 126

The students present in the National institutions numbered 10,500

The professors and teachers, who resigned from government colleges, numbered 76."[10]

The meaning by it that when on large scale the peasantry's participation, in the Non-cooperation and Khilafat movement, came into being in the form of active cooperation in United Provinces then the results, of the sort mentioned above, began to appear because in it a new form of zeal was there. We can imagine, the peasantry's enthusiasm and strength provided by it to the Non-cooperation movement, from the civil disobedience movement begun by Gandhiji ten years after it in 1930 in which the peasants had given a new direction to the movement especially in United Provinces. The peasants of United Provinces had certainly understood themselves that by this time their class did not know its might. Also it was grievous matter really that the peasantry, the source to bring up all, lived miserable life and remained encircled by exploitation and miseries. The peasants had firmly taken some following determinations and under the direction and leadership of Nehru they had acted upon these and sacrificed a lot for the sake of national interest –

(a) Because the strength of the peasants lies in their number of crores and even bigger than it their might is their labour, so, they should not show weakness before tyrant and if there is any weakness anywhere, having removed it the political power is to be taken over;

(b) Till the peasants organisation will not gradually grow and enlarge by then the peasantry will remain oppressed. If the peasants want themselves their welfare, they will have to take their organisation on the path of strengthening and they will have to create the feeling of affection for each other within their class. It will have to understand, "the peasants as a whole are the son of a father";

(c) Because without arousing feeling of self grandeur among the peasants there cannot be their welfare and because they feel that the other persons are bigger and mightier than them and they are unfortunate and weaker, therefore, they will have to adopt self-grandness. And it will have to accept that the peasant, who commits minimum sin, meets his livings through hard labour, who is not a least dependent on others; so, he should not take himself lightly;

(d) The peasant should make up his mind that to claim his right and justice he needs not to apply or request, through the might of his strength he will have to do all that; and

(e) The peasantry will have to remove from upon themselves the prints of slavery of moneylender, landlord or government courtier classes. They will have to abandon to hang on somebody's lips, be ever prepared to face hardships but the negation will have to be defeated.

## The Civil disobedience movement and the peasantry

In April, 1930, Mahatma Gandhi lifted a handful of salt from the sea coast of Dandi and commenced the Salt Satyagraha. He was rounded up on May 5 and in between this period the civil disobedience movement spread throughout the country. Though the violation of Salt Act through making salt was declared its chief basis, yet behind the movement the reality was to get Swaraj (self government). So, where the Salt Act violation on large scale came into being, the peasantry under the leadership of Congress Party opened in it such chapter that it came in the movement's forefront. In Bombay and Central Provinces the people violated the Forest Act through cutting trees. The peasantry vowed not to pay levy or rent in Gujarat, Bengal and Central Provinces. But United Provinces only was such state in reality where the peasantry, not to pay the rent, commenced the agitation rampantly, fastly and influentially. This movement was associated with the Civil Disobedience Movement and within it to be found the political peasants movement and their internal relations were the consequences of Nehru's principle and conduct entirely. After a week of the violation of the Salt Act, or on 14 April, 1930 Pandit Jawaharlal Nehru was arrested and he was sent in Naini Central prison. This time Nehru, who too was President of the Congress, was worried of the country's circumstances especially political situation and the peasants conditions. After the Lahore Congress he could not get so much time that he might take the common people, the peasantry having directed it properly in the Satyagraha being carried on then for National independence. Really he wished it, "As the peasantry in 1920-21, during the Non-cooperation movement especially in United Provinces had provided the Gandhiji's programme with the strength which it got never before, let this class be prepared to sacrifice this time even on more larger scale than that one in order to end its miseries." It was the cause that he, on 17 January, 1930, having picturised beautifully in an article 'The Salt Satyagraha and situation of the peasantry' which was published in *The Hindustan Times* edition of 20 January, 1930, wrote, "among the increased taxes 20 per cent heavy increase is imposed on the peasants in the form of rent and 3 per cent in Salt tax." These both are nothing except making lame the countryside India and the peasantry. For detail see appendix number 5.

During the Civil Disobedience Movement on 16 August, 1930, as Panditji was released, he got chance of implementing his certain principle of associating the peasantry with the political movement. Nehru himself had admitted in his self story.[14]

As it is already mentioned that since the commencement of the Civil Disobedience Movement in addition of the United Provinces the peasants of Gujarat and Bengal provinces had started the non-payment of rent movement but among it the stronger movement was in some parts of Gujarat and it gradually grew which was fully in sight of Nehru but it had lost its political character though in the begining of the Civil Disobedience Movement it was a part of it. The main cause behind becoming the political movement was the system of land, except some parts (one or two areas) in Gujarat there was Raiyyatvari system directly linked with the government and the movement against the rent meant direct confrontation against the government. Due to it the peasants struggle having hidden its original face became naturally a political movement against the government. The other was the situation of United Provinces, it was at once different from Gujarat in the form that here the peasantry through its agitation could not directly influence the government. In between the government and the peasantry there were the landlords and Taluqdars. In case if the peasantry stopped the payment of rent, it could directly influence not the government but this class (intermediatry one). So, Nehru wished to stir the peasants movement in a special form and that too in this form that where it might become decisive in the process of fundamental change in the country's political circumstances there its own character could be maintained. In between these circumstances the implementation of the principle was very difficult task but Nehru efficiently could do all that.

Having assessed the political and economic circumstances, Pandit Nehru, for the sake of commencing the peasantry movement in the countryside, convened a conference of the peasant representatives on 19 October, 1930 in Allahabd district in which 1600 representatives participated. This conference decided to agitate immediately through the non-payment of rent, commenced on 20 October, 1930. This struggle remained continued during the period of the Civil disobedience movement, the Salt Satyagraha and it having maintained its own recognition provided the Salt Satyagraha with huge strength. Its leader Nehru, while telling again and again the Salt Satyagraha as an object to end miseries of the peasantry throughout the province, arranged participation of the villagers in it and in accordance with the expectation, having beautifully coordinated the political movement with the peasants movement, presented a new way for the coming generations. To produce here some instances of his calls will not be irrelevant. At a place Nehru said, "Under every condition, being organised under the Congress's flag the peasants should fight the British imperialism. Without change of the system, as it is obvious from the object of the Salt Satyagraha, the peasant cannot get liberation from his oppression. Finally the welfare can be brought about by the Swaraj."[15]

Accordingly at another place Nehru insistently said, "Having become organised the peasants will have to provide their strength to the Congress and the movement being stirred by it." And it too will have to be given not only to get ease from some miseries but to attain the Swaraj, the solution of national problem and subsequent four cornered development. While sending the report of his call to the Home Ministry of Government of India, a C.I.D. Officer wrote, "According to his charter of demands he (Pandit Nehru) wants organised and equal strength of the peasantry throughout the country so that it may become the chief base of strength of the Congress in National struggle."[16]

## The influence and cooperation of the peasants struggle upon political movement of the Salt Satyagraha

The influence of the peasants movement commenced at the call of Jawaharlal Nehru in United Provinces and its contribution in the Salt Satyagraha cannot anyhow be minimized in its assessment. "In March, 1931, in Allahabad district alone 20 meetings which were held in political form, out of these 17 were concerned with the question of non-payment of rent by the peasants. The situation of countryside was extremely serious and any time what could happen anywhere could not be imagined."[17] It was stated by the C.I.D. report of United Provinces itself which was released on 28 March, 1931. Not only it but the Kisan Sabhas too became so stronger and mightier that these also made the peasants undaunted and definitely the fear of landlords and police got reduced. The District Magistrate of Mathura on 27 March, 1931, to the Commissioner of Agra Commissionery, wrote, "The meetings of Kisan Sabha are going on regularly and this propaganda of the Congress is getting successful that provide the Congress with strength and defeat the government. In Mathura Tehsil a Congressman has been appointed Tehsildar; under Farah police station in a village a Congress Police Station is established. The villagers are being inspired to come in the Congress's court in place of the general courts. They (the peasants) are informed if they will not be satisfied from the verdicts of the court, from Mathura a representative of the Congress will come to settle the dispute."[18]

Thus, it so appeared as if the peasants at several places, through making the parallel governments, failed the government and provided the Congress's political movement with huge strength. Though at some places the peasantry became out of control and inclined towards violence, yet it was against the principles of Gandhiji and Nehru. The circumstances had become so horrible, according to a District Magistrate, "One or two days back a petty landlord from Sadabad Tehsil during talking has told me that he fears the atmosphere has now become equivalent to that of 1857. This analysis of the circumstances by a petty landlord shows that by which thinking process the countryside is being directed."[19]

The example of fearlessness from the landlords and police, we can derive well from the report of Home Secretary, Jagdish Prasad of United Provinces on 22 April, 1931. In the report to the Home Secretary of the Government of India, it was written, "On 28 March, the occupant tenant peasants, who were refusing to pay rent, tried to assault Dildar Hussain, a famous and major landlord of Sujawalpur village under Bilhore police station. On 30 March a wealthy landlord of Birhan namely Thakur Chitar Singh was assaulted in Bargaon near Fatehpur border under Kakvan police station and he in serious condition was taken to hospital. He too was passing through specific circumstances due to the non-payment of rent movement."[20]

The countryside had become the centre of perfect awakening and the peasantry's movement getting linked with the political movement, 'had proved this fact that the battle of independence commenced from the cities had gone to the countryside. Specially the struggle of United Provinces, which was led by Jawaharlal Nehru, had carried such mighty, latest and wonderful consequences. Nehru himself has also accepted this influential fact as steady truth.'[21] According to the government data '65,600 persons went to prison in the first round of the Civil Disobedience Movement (The Salt Satyagraha) and in accordance with the sources of the Congress working committee about 75,000 persons were jailed but among them there was majority of the peasants and villagers. As far as the United Provinces was concerned, there 75 per cent arrested persons were the peasants who had participated in the peasants agitation of non-payment of rent with the Civil Disobedience Movement.'[22]

'It should be the right of common persons to govern the country. Every common person may appoint its pleasure; so, to attain the Swaraj is the first national requirement. Till the foreign exploiters and their Indian mediators, the oppressors of their own countrymen under their individual interests, as landlords, moneylenders, Taluqdars will not become existenceless, by then the producer of wealth from the land and its (land's) true son, the peasant, how will get the breath of relief? With this conviction of thinking Nehru, for the same of country's future and with it associated the socio-economic aspects and no-rent struggle being stirred for the sake of the peasants' existence or against exploitation and oppression, saw these mutually connected and gave them practical shape. In this context he had told the peasantry clearly, "We want the Swaraj (self government). For the Swaraj we have commenced this struggle (the Salt Satyagraha) and numerous Hindu and Muslim peasants too helpted us fully in it. They know well that finally they will be benefited by it and their miseries-difficulties will come to an end. He called upon for help because the real Swaraj means, as they know, end of miseries and poverty. Who are the country's people? They are not a few city-dwellers or professional lawyers but they are the peasants, the inhabitants of villages. When there will be no end of the peasantry's miseries, what the Swaraj will be meant for? The Swaraj's true meaning is common people – the end of the peasantry's miseries in context of rent or ejectment from land or their other forms also. Such Swaraj will keep them away from any sort of misery. The Swaraj means not any sort of foreign rule and in individual capacity not becoming of any king or emperor or governor to be the ruler of the people. Our Swaraj means a Panchayati Raj (the rule of local bodies of the villages) for the country, where there will be no distinction between the people and the ruler and in it all the ruled will become the rulers. From here there will be an end of miseries. So, the peasantry's struggle for its existence means to get the Swaraj and to take over the government in its hands. So, the Salt Satyagraha – struggle for the independence – and No-rent Movement of the peasants are the two coins of an aspect."[23]

## The Quit India Movement and the peasantry's participation

From commencing of the Oudh peasants movement Jawaharlal Nehru dedicated his day-today deeds and thoughts for the peasantry and when in 1936, under his presidentship the conference of the Congress held at Lucknow, for the first time it allowed the Kisan Sabha within its organisational structure. It was in brief the proposal of this Congress, "The Congress is of the opinion that before the nation the most urgent and significant problem is of poverty, unemployment and the condition of the peasants, behind which the fundamental cause is the system of land and the situation of rent etc. So, the Congress demands the organisational freedom of the farm labourers and the peasants. It demands the security of the peasants, equitable re-arrangement of land and re-assessment of rent, help full of honesty and their protection from the land owners and landlords."[24] For details see appendix 2.

After this proposal Nehru got associated with the Kisan Sabha on national level and the peasantry then in the country became more active due to his calling upon. In Bihar under the leadership of Swami Sahajanand, who had been the national president of the Kisan Sabha after its formation, the peasantry's struggle against rent and Bhawali system, in 1939 the struggle and organisation of the United Provinces' peasants against landlord system which was led by Jawaharlal Nehru himself and in 1938, combating of the Andhra Pradesh peasants against landlord system etc. examples can be mentioned for it. Though Nehru struggled more for the peasantry in United Provinces, yet because all over the country it was commonly oppressed; so, for the proposal, of abolition of common oppression, to be presented in the Congress, he played important role. Its result was that in 1942, during the Quit India Movement the peasantry did not leave any stone unturned having assessed its class interests protected in the country's freedom and accepting of the leadership of the Indian National Congress. "The Government's data tell that commenced on 9 August, 1942, in this leaderless Quit India Movement 64000 persons were sent to prison."[25] But "the sources of Indian National Congress had stated that about 1,25,000 persons were arrested."[26] But whatever it may be, among these arrests the rural peasants were the foremost. "In the first two months or in August and

September, 1942, in accordance with the sources of the Congress, out of 15,000 persons dead due to police and army firing, 70 to 80 per cent were actually the peasants, villagers or workers."[27] It was the result of zeal of the rural people and its longing of getting the freedom that during this struggle it disconnected "318 railway stations and 12,000 telephone and wireless centres and did derailing at 59 places."[28] In the previous month 'the government had recovered a crore of rupees in form of punishment from the rural masses of the people. These people, the peasants, were the enthusiasts of the freedom.'[29] And thus Jawaharlal Nehru was foremost among the creators of this love or enthusiasm. The symbol of his efforts and labour the All India Kisan Sabha's membership, "at the time of commencement of the Quit India Movement, was eight lacs and these eight lacs peasants in spite of being affiliated with the peasants organisation also were the soldiers of the battle for freedom."[30]

Thus we get the conclusion that the mass leader Pandit Jawaharlal Nehru endeavoured ceaselessly for the peasantry's participation foremostly in the battle of the country's freedom and this endeavour in his country is found in form of sentimentality or emotionality as the sentiment for the progress of the peasantry. He had got the certain and simultaneously proper conviction that most of the peasantry's problems were due to the British imperialist rule and if we, getting emancipated from the foreign rule, formed the democratic government of our own; these problems could be solved. For example through the democratic government by the pressure of majority the landlord system would be abolished. Due to the self restraint the people would not be terrified of the police and law. But this would not be done in presence of the foreign government, whose basis was the strength. So, the first condition was the end of this rule of slavery. In accordance with his supposition the peasantry came in the struggle for National independence and wherever there was weakness in the sharpness of the struggle for National independence, it was accomplished by the peasants as in 1920-21, in United Provinces and they raised higher the flag of independence. At other places the peasantry provided the battle for independence with strength. Nehru had learnt it through studying the problems of peasantry that the struggles of the peasants and for independence might be accumulated to secure the result of double benefit, *i.e.* the country's independence and the peasantry's consciousness. Then its double benefit would be seen during the construction of new India, *i.e.* the self-reliance and progress of agriculture sector and growth of standard of living in the villages.

The above-mentioned ideological policy of Nehru and practice of accumulating the political struggle with the peasantry really played very important role for the country's destiny. The peasants could do welfare of both their own and the country.

## References

1. Home Department Political 1931, No. 33/11, N.A.I., New Delhi.
2. "Rae Bareli has done a lot, still more is expected from Rae Bareli. Our peace is still far away. The more our strength increases the sooner. We will have real peace and this is only possible when we obtain (Purna) Complete Swaraj. I, therefore, hope that all tenants brethren will understand what has been done and what still remains to be done. We can not take rest yet we will take rest only when the troubles of tenants are over. That time will also come." Home Department Political 1931, F. No. 31/XI, N.A.I., New Delhi.
3. Antonova K.A. and others, History of India, Moscow, U.S.S.R., 1984, p. 554.
4. *Ibid.*
5. Kumar, Dr. Ravindra, Contribution of Maulana Azad in solving the Problem of Communalism and the National Liberation Movement of India, Muzaffar Nagar, 1988, p. 2-8.
6. Home Political 1921, F. No. 2/13, N.A.I., New Delhi.
7. History of India, Moscow, U.S.S.R., p. 557.
8. *Ibid.*, p. 554.
9. *Ibid.*, p. 556.
10. Young India, edited by Mahatma Gandhi, Navjeevan Press, Ahmedabad, August 11, 1921.
11. Kumar Dr. Ravindra, Maulana Azad's role in, p. 2-8.
12. *Ibid.*
13. Hindustan Times, New Delhi, January 20, 1930, p. 1.
14. "It seemed an ideal opportunity for a no-tax campaign, both as a part of the General Civil Disobedience Movement and, independently, on its own merits. It was manifestly impossible both for landlords and tenants to pay up the full demand out of that year's produce. They had to fall back on old reserves, if they had any, or borrow." – Nehru, J.L. An Autobiography, p. 231.
15. Home Department Political 1930, F.No. 4/8 ((205), National Archives of India, New Delhi.

16. Home Political 1930, No. 5575. (Report of the State Government of U.P., Lucknow/ P.A. Lucknow.
17. "Out of 20 meetings reported from the Allahabad District, 17 were in connection with the question of non-payment of rent, and the situation in the villages is regarded as extremely critical, and serious outbreaks may occur at any moment. There is very general idea that Congress is now Government, and tenants are refusing to deal with Zamindars or with officials and are referring everything to Congress. Reference to the serious effects of the continuance of propaganda, while the police are unable to take action, are made by many Districts, and it is believed that to resume eventual control of the situation will be difficult. In Rae Bareli Congressmen as representatives of tenants, not the taluqdars, but no compromise on the subject of remission of rent was reached. It is likely that the Congress people, who at present are obliged to find some outlet for their energies and are exploiting the rent problem, will be unable to control the tenants, and that widespread violence will result. Taluqdars can with good reasons point out that they are unable to pay their revenue in view of the propaganda and the withdrawal of Government help." (C.I.D. Report – U.P.) March 28, 1931., Home Department Political, F. No. 33/34/31., N.A.I., New Delhi.
18. Home Political 1931, F. No. 33/31., N.A.I., New Delhi.
19. *Ibid.*
20. *Ibid.*
21. "The No-tax Campaign in the United Provinces had one important result so far as the province was concerned. It shifted the centre of gravity of our struggle from the urban to the rural areas, and it thereby revitalised the movement and put it on a broader and more enduring basis. Though our city people became bored and tired, and our middle class workers were obviously rather stale, the movement itself in U.P. was as strong, or even stronger, than it had been at any other time. In other provinces this change over from urban to rural, from political to economic issues, did not take place to the same extent, and consequently they continued to be dominated by the cities and to suffer increasing from the weariness of the middle class elements. Even the City of Bombay, which had all along played a prominent part in the movement, began to grow a little stale. Defiance of authority would go on there and elsewhere, and assert would continue, but all this seemed somewhat artificial. The organic element had gone. This was natural though as it is impossible to keep the masses at a certain revolutionary pitch long periods. Ordinarily this was a question of days, but Civil Disobedience had the remarkable capacity for lengthening this period to many months, and even then of carrying on at a lower pitch for an indefinite period." – Nehru Pt. Jawahar Lal, An Autobiography.
22. Kumar, Dr. Ravindra, Contribution of Maulana Abul Kalam Azad, ....page 12.
23. Home Department Political 1930, F. No. 32 and K.W. National Archives of India, New Delhi.
24. Home Political 1936, F. No. 4/8/36., National Archives of India, New Delhi.

25. Guha, Shri A.C., India's Struggle Quarter of a Century, Publication Division 1982, New Delhi., p. 501.
26. Kumar, Dr. Ravindra, Contribution of Maulana Azad, p. 2-18.
27. Guha,. Shri A.C. India's Struggle Quarter of a Century, 1982, p. 502.
28. *Ibid.*, p. 501.
29. Antonova, K.A. and others, History of India, Moscow, U.S.S.R., 1984, p. 635.
30. *Ibid.*

## CHAPTER IV

# Nehru's views on Landlords and Taluqdars and his impressions on the evils of Zamindari system

**(A) Nehru : Indian National Congress and Zamindars**

**(B) The hurdles faced by Nehru in the implementation of his ideas**

Jawaharlal Nehru was acquainted with each and every kind of condition, deeds or conducts of the landlords or Taluqdars. And as he expressed his ideas clearly about the evils of landlord system, its other instance is not available with his counterparts of his age. How much clear he was about the landlord system, it could be imagined from his this clear sentence, "Today I say obviously that the landlord system is the biggest evil of our country and its complete abolition is essential for the construction of new India. Till this system based on exploitation is not ended, social justice and economic progress cannot even be imagined."

### Landlords and Nehru

Nehru, while thinking over the term 'landlord' and its real state (condition), has said,

"In the ryotwari provinces it (Zamindar) means the peasant proprietor. Even in the typical Zamindari provinces, it includes in its fold the relatively few big landlords, thousands of middle landowners, and hundreds of thousands of persons who live in the extreme poverty are no better than tenants. In the United Provinces, so far as I can remember, there are a million and a half persons classed as zamindars. Probably over ninety per cent of these are almost on the same level as the poorest tenants, and another nine per cent are only moderately well off. The biggish landowners are not more than five thousand in the whole province, and of this number about one-tenth might be considered the really big Zamindars and taluqdars. In some instances the bigger tenants are better off than the destitute petty landlords. Both these poor landowners and the middle landlords, though often intellectually backward, are as a whole a fine body of men and women, and, with proper education and training can be made into excellent citizens. They have taken a considerable part in the nationalist movement. Not so the taluqdars and the big zamindars, barring a few notable exceptions. They have not even the virtues of an aristocracy. As a class they are physically and intellectually degenerate and have outlived their day; they will continue only so long as an external power like the British Government props them up."

In other states (provinces) where different landlord system exists, there also thousands merely are the landowners of the middle class and the rest lacs and crores of people are there, who live below the poverty line, whose condition is not better than that of the tenants who were found in the system of United Provinces. The meaning by it that the landlord happened to be the owner of the peasants and he used to let the land to the peasants. The maximum rent, beyond the certain assessment, recovery of rent was compulsory. In this recovery the police force was generally used. And according to Nehru, "The landlords and Taluqdars were natural leaders of the people. And with them the landowners felt proudness while accepting them to be the imposed leaders or owners of the peasantry. Simultaneously they felt arrogance of being heirs of the British rule. The British government itself used to give them special teaching and apprised them of the government's presence."[2] The Taluqdars, landlords or landowners enjoyed special privileges, to recover rent, to employ someone in service without remuneration or to attach instead of and to ejact or to confiscate. All it had yielded the biggest evil that, "India (Indian society) bifurcated into two parts. The first part contained the landlords, landowners and Taluqdars, the other part included the tenants (peasants), sub-tenant peasants and agricultural labourers."[3] This situation we do not assess not only according to Uttar Pradesh (then United Provinces) but Nehru himself, "for the whole of the country, has accepted this analysis."[4] This division into two parts was inhuman and uncivilised from the point of view of humanity and God. The meaning by it that the existence of artificial distinction between the two human beings made of the same soil. Among them there was a ruler (native or countrymade) and the other was ruled. This protected landlord class was not only guilty for dividing the society but it depended upon telling a lie in order to preserve its existence and luxurious life and branded this lie as a truth. For example, "short term tenancy, can be cited, which was prevalent mostly in the eastern districts of United Provinces. The landowner was addicted of not giving receipt of rent and always used to tell a lie that he had not yet received rent." On the basis of this lie he felt proudness of maintaining his power (existence) or superiority also. "The tenant had not any reply of his (landlords's) lie and neither there was any way out and also to transform this lie into truth." So, in this system there was considerable evil and Jawaharlal Nehru wanted to end this evil which was only possible through abolition of this system. And for it the end of foreign government was essential.

Taluqdari system, being of upper level than landlord system, was also in the same form (exploiting form). The meaning by it that landlord was parasite on the peasantry and was its owner while Taluqdar was parasite on the landlords. The example of evil of this system is quoted – the Taluqdars used to receive their heavy expenses from their subordinates. "Expense of marriage in their families, expense of boy's education in the foreign country, expense of functions held on the arrival of the Governor or higher officers and expense of motor car or elephant etc. for their own use, all these expenses were to be borne by the subordinates of Taluqdars."[5] Now as it was natural that finally the poor peasant was oppressed by it and his blood was to be sucked. Nehru had hatred for this system and accepted that there was economic exploitation in this system. In fact it was the result of this countrywide bad system that, "this class (the peasantry), having representation of more than 75 per cent people, the poor peasants, named merely peasant. He (the peasant) had no base for his livelihood. Neither he had his own money, nor he had land. Only he had his labour on the basis of which the landlord and the Taluqdar were having luxury."[6]

Thus, there were numerous other evils in the landlord system, due to which Nehru had developed in his mind a certain thinking about it whose final target was the 'abolition of Zamindari system and providing the landholding rights on the land being tilled by it to the peasantry who had been groaning for centuries under the yoke of slavery.' Later on Nehru too endeavoured ceaselessly for it. For example in 1952, 'Uttar Pradesh government abolished Zamindari system and immediately one crore peasants became landowners themselves.'[7] How much desirous Nehru had been for this step to be taken? Its imagination is not possible. The same policy was adopted all over the country. Where it was necessary to abolish the Zamindari system there it was done through enactment and at rest of the places the Land Reforms Acts were enacted.

How much bad in fact this system was? Under the 'Permanent Land Settlement Bill' of 'Lord Cornwalis', two-third of the land of United Provinces was the property of landlords belonging upper castes who never tilled the land and inhumanly ate the hard begotten earnings of the crores of peasants, farm labourers (sub-peasants) and lived luxurious life.'[8]

## Nehru, the Congress party and the Landlord class

To achieve the goal of independence Nehru was prepared to get cooperation of all those classes who were willing for it, even the Taluqdar and landlord classes. It was the reason then inside the Congress Party especially in United Provinces and Gujarat Nehru happened to be close to several landlord class leaders. For instance we can cite – In United Provinces Mr. Shervani, in Gujarat Kanjibhai Desai and Darbargopal Das Desai. Nehru had seen these leaders turning from the landlord mentality to further the class interests of peasantry and towards the country's independence.

Nehru knew it, as he has himself written in his 'self story', "My chief activities, however, lay in the United Provinces where the agrarian situation absorbed Congress attention. The U.P. Provincial Congress Committee consisted of over a hundred and fifty members, and met every two or three months. Its executive council, consisting of about fifteen members, met frequently and was incharge of its agrarian department. In the second half of the year 1931, a special agrarian committee was appointed by this council. It is interesting to find that several zamindars were prominently associated with the Council and this committee through, and all steps were taken with their approval. Indeed, the president of our provincial committee for the year (and consequently the *ex-officio* head of the executive council and the Agrarian Committee) was Tasadduq Ahmad Khan Sherwani, who belongs to a well known Zamindari family. The General Secretary, Sri Prakasha, as well as several leading members of the Council were also Zamindari families. The remaining members were middle class professional people. There was not a single member, from tenant or poor peasant class in our provincial committee. Peasant were to be found in our district committee." So a such co-operant trifigure came forward which might not only unclash its efforts for the country's independence but it could be effective for the progress and prosperity of the peasantry. This trifigure included leadership, the Congress organisation and landlord class. The landlord class, which was mainly cooperating the Congress for National independence was occupying posts of the Congress organisation. From it there was expectation of cooperating the peasantry also. Jawaharlal Nehru moved ahead this thinking in spite of its primary evils and it yielded good results not only in United Provinces but in Punjab, Bihar, Orissa, Bengal and Gujarat. Firstly the basis of these results was the participation of innumerable landlords in the activities of the Congress even without caring for their landlordships, supporting of Gandhiji's programmes by them wholeheartedly and becoming of them very liberal towards their tenants – the peasantry. It was a great achievement.

"Darbargopal Das Desai, a big landlord for the sake of country, sacrificed his landlordship and regency of 'Dhasa' in Saurashtra region of Gujarat and he accompanied by his wife namely Bhaktiba Desai jumped in the battle for independence." Another very big landlord of Olpad region namely Kanaihyalal Desai, having associated himself with the Congress organisation and Mahatma Gandhi, "not only practised perfect liberality for his occupant tenant peasants but never recovered anything against the will of his tenants."[11] Later on, Kanjibhai Desai's this point of view developed that the peasantry ought to be made self-reliant and in 1937, he himself produced the matter of Land Reforms Act before the Bombay government and subsequently bore the full responsibility of implementing it (Act).[12] In Bihar, in 1937-38, many landlords through their liberal conduct proposed to end the Bhawali system and liberalisation of the land Act."[13] Such happenings had been there in other provinces too.

'If the landlords, having adopted flexibility, wish to serve a least or more the interests of peasants and while working simultaneously for the Swaraj through participating in the programmes of the Congress, it will be pleasurable and significant. In the two forms – firstly, the progress (keeping money in sight) of the strength of national liberation movement and secondly, the strengthening of Party organisation with the cooperation and economic help of the upper class.' These two forms had been of the point of view of Jawahar Lal Nehru. This point of view came into being not due to principle but from his own conduct. "In the beginning of Nehru's public life when he himself was the secretary of Allahabad District Congress Committee under the presidentship of Purshottam Das Tandon, he found that in that committee there was sympathy for the peasantry in spite of the presence of landlords in it. So, the landlord, even being landlord by nature, can think sympathetically for the peasantry."[14]

Not only so, but in 1930, the Congress Committee of United Provinces had formed a special council. The present secretary and members of this peasant council were the landlords or came from upper classes but this council had led the non-payment of rent agitation of the peasants and it had done better work for the peasants in the regions of Allahabad district and Oudh having landlord system and Taluqdari system respectively."[15] Simultaneously knowing of it will be amazing that Allahabd was the district having the best Congress organisation throughout the United Provinces. The reason of it was that the political activities had gained momentum in Allahabad city and the persons of organisation were visiting the villages while assessing the circumstances but the foremost in the organisation the persons of middle class were especially from landlord class."[16] And it is well known fact that Allahabad had sounded trumpet of the emancipation of peasantry in Oudh. Nehru had several times accepted the landlord class as helpful in practice from the social and human point of view and he did the work of link between the Congress and the landlords even while criticising evils of this system and openly opposing it. In 1931, Pandit Nehru had put forth plan of working in the form of the peasants union (Kisan Union), within the Congress organisation for the peasants to attain economic justice, in which non-peasants and controlled landlords were also to be included. And in this work he had entirely willing to show to the government that they (the Congressmen) were not doing every work with political motive."[17]

Behind the moving accompanied by the Congress and the landlord class, Nehru had put forth also an important argument that the battle which the Congress was fighting for the peasantry, it was really and finally not serving the own interest of foreign imperialist government. That (the government) provided the landlords with the chance of exploiting their own country's people while it also exploited the landlords. So, if the peasants were advised to boycott the landlords and not to pay them revenue, the same way the landlords could be asked. Meaning by it that the landlords ought to boycott the government and they should not pay the government tax. Thus the peasants and the landlords would be rescued from unnecessary burden laden upon both of them. The purposes of both would become closer. The foreign economic interest would come to an end. To practise it, Nehru in 1930, in non-payment of rent agitation, commenced during the Civil Disobedience Movement, the appeal which he had delivered, it was for both – the peasants and the landlords. According to the appeal, "In practice, the landlords who pay revenue to the government, among them numerous are sympathetic towards the national liberation movement. They are under heavy pressure and thus they have to loose a lot. The tenant peasantry is now firm not to pay revenue and its agitation has turned into Non-payment of Rent Movement. The situation is dangerous not only in Allahabad district but throughout the whole of United Provinces. The peasantry has made up its mind firmly not to pay rent. Neither the government nor the landlords can deviate the peasants in spite of their efforts for months. In the two forms the peasants are standing mentally prepared to struggle. On the one hand in the political form they are in the Civil Disobedience Movement, on the other hand they are in the peasants movement in the economic form. Under such circumstances the landlord class should prove its affection for its motherland. They (the landlords) should have friendship with their peasants. They should feel their miseries. Through doing so, they will not be loosing anything rather they will be gaining. To achieve the national independence, they are duty bound to do whatever they can and this time may become example provided the duty is fulfilled."[18] From this appeal it is evident that how Nehru wished the cooperation and co-working from the landlord class. He liked the cooperation of landlord class to meet the purpose and for it he did the best work.

In this work Nehru at that itme stood successful. At that time how much importance of his thinking and conduct had been there, more than that it is today. At that time as the peasantry had hardships and it was victim of landlord class's exploitation, the same way, though not having such serious condition, yet the condition of agricultural labourers required to be reformed and the peasantry should adopt the positive policy of co-working with the labourers. To root out injustice and everybody might get equal chance of progress was the purpose of Nehru and that purpose he had used as rapport between the Congress and the landlords. If Nehru remained anxious to take the landlords in the mainstream of nation, simultaneously there was bad smell of huge evils of landlord system in his feeling and he was desirous to root out these (evils). That was why he had done more work in the peasantry to make the peasants mightier than doing the work for Congress organisation. For it there had been this argument that if the Congress any time avoided to take steps for the peasants or the circumstances did not allow it to do so, the peasants should have been so mightier to do it. It had so happened in 1932, as Subhas Chandra Bose had written that, "the peasants had evidently told the Congress that if it would not commence no-rent movement, Kisan League (the peasants league) itself would commence that movement. Therefore, the Congress Committee decided to commence it."[19] The comment of Subhas Baboo is given in the references.[20]

Nehru gave priority to solve the agricultural problems and he never adopted the policy of cooperation with landlords at the cost of compromising on the norms of the interests of peasantry or he never had the policy of taking the landlord class close to the Congress organisation. For strong example can be quoted the period of 1931, when Gandhi-Irwin Pact had taken place and where on the one hand the Civil Disobedience Movement had been adjourned, there on the other hand the non-payment of rent movement under the Kisan Sabha organisation was also ceased. But Nehru knew it that the economic circumstances of the peasants were more complicated than the political movement. From these circumstances the peasants required to be relieved. So, Nehru had said, "In United Provinces the basis of rent being realized from the peasants should be accepted the prices (commodities and crops). The purpose of saying is that there should be abatement of rent in the same ratio as the prices of commodities are down and its base year should be accepted this year 1931. The conditon of 1931 concerning the price index is the same as it was thirty years back in 1901. Never the condition was so serious as it is today and it is for all the peasant landowners, non-landowner peasants or sub-peasants. The equitable solution of the peasants problems is that the tenant should pay rent on the basis of his cost of production and income. The other important task is that of ceiling of land and this probelm exists for the peasants as a whole of the country not only for United Provinces peasants. These are the tested problems in practice and it is truth that these problems cannot be overlooked. Neither the peasants can be left in the lurch to be sacrificed on the altar of these problems."[21]

We come to the conclusion that Nehru's scale of co-operation or non-cooperation between the landlord class and the Indian National Congress was definitely the country's independence but he never tolerated reduction in the peasantry's interest. He knew it, as the the Governor of United Provinces, Sir Henry Hague too had said that the British government by hook or crook wanted to maintain the landlord system and for its sake it shut its eyes on having seen oppressions by the landlord class upon the peasantry.[22] The cause was quite obvious that if there would be no landlord class and the man in street would move towards becoming self-reliant economically, how the existence of British government would be safe ? So, the interest of the government lied in the existence of this system and the indirect terror of it to be placed upon the people. Then numerous well known persons of the landlord class while having adopted the liberal policy had become not only attracted towards the Congress programmes for the country's independence but they had perfectly adopted these in spite of the fact that their tendency was not yet fully clear and they had not yet changed their nature completely. How the spontaneous cooperation of such landlords could be refused? In spite of being a staunch socialist and well-wisher of the peasantry Jawaharlal Nehru moved ahead taking them (the landlords) with due to this cause. Though he faced not only difficulties while implementing fully his ideology regarding the land and its relations with the peasants, the landlord system and its abolition, yet he could not practise it well even but he never deviated from his norm. And his firmness we find in the material form in his this statement, "Our real purpose is to make sit the peasantry on reverential place of which it is really rightful. The peasants and the villagers are the owners, producers and nurturers of the cultural inheritance of this country, not this landlord class and the persons of upper class."[23]

## The difficulties confronted by Nehru

In 1936, the conference of the Congress under the presidentship of Jawaharlal Nehru himself held at Lucknow. It held under the changed political circumstances. The Civil Disobedience Movement – No-rent Campaign in the United Provinces of 1930, prior Bardoli peasants Satyagraha of 1928 and the same way wave among the peasants in all the provinces – all these could turn the political situation of the country. Though not a talk to say yet these movements had bestowed the matchless strength to the Congress organisation and national liberation movement on the one hand and on the other hand weakened the situation of the landlords, landowners and Taluqdars also. But in spite of it too there was no leaning towards the problem of peasantry according to the will of Nehru in the Lucknow Conference of the Congress. The C.I.D. of government had confirmed this fact.[24] Nehru's special insistence was on the peasants problem during this conference and it was to be noted that in it for the first time a firm proposal for the peasants was also passed as it is mentioned in appendix No. 2 in the end. But it was very unfortunate for Nehru that in 1936, there was difference in the Congress on the questions of the organisation of Kisan Sabha and to get sanctioned equitable rights to the peasants.[25]

Several times it so happened when he remained in troubles while implementing his ideology regarding the welfare of peasantry in spite of his sincere willing. Such happenings not only ocurred in pre-independence days but in post-independence days too. In 1947-49, in some parts of the country uprose peasants movements. Among these the biggest struggles were of the different masses of poor tenant peasants who were demanding abatement of rent, reform in rent system and the rights of their appropriate freedom. Secondly, such type of struggles were commenced by the occupant tenant peasants of West Bengal, Bihar, Bombay and Punjab etc. provinces. But Nehru felt trouble while implementing his pro-peasant policy in order to provide the peasants with justice who were victims of illegal timely and untimely ejectment by the landlords and landowners. Several times he passed through such troubles.

In fact Nehru was a socialist thinker. And the chief basis of his socialism was – the country's circumstances accompanied by three main factors. These factors were – "Planning, economic development and socialist system. For him, without economic development there was not any socialism, without planning there was not any economic development and without development of economic sector there was no progress."[26] Nehru yearned to see the progress of peasantry and development of agriculture sector in accordance with his ideological line. It was the reason that "where he after independence advocated the land reforms to be implemented effectively there he favoured agriculture work to be done through getting it included in industrial sector."[27] But due to numerous troubles, difficulties and circumstances he could not do it and according to his will he could not utilise the Constituent Assembly even.

Nehru had been anxious to take the peasants on large scale in the Cooperative Movement simultaneously with the land reforms and the post-independence nation moved also in this direction in accordance with his will but not in the same form and not on the same scale how much he wished. Even then the nation progressed unprecedentedly in the field of grains production and behind it there had been the great contribution of Nehru. He had been of the firm opinion about conducting the peasantry's matters in context of India that "the political democracy without being accompanied by the economic freedom cannot get its true base and the poverty of common person in the country cannot be eradicated without the economic revolution and socialist system."

## References


1. Nehru, Pt. Jawaharlal, An Autobiography, p. 50.
2. Amar Ujala (Daily) Meerut, 20.1.88.
3. Home Department Political 1929, F. No. 12/29., National Archives of India, New Delhi.
4. Nehru, Pt. Jawaharlal, An Autobiography, p. 52.
5. *Ibid.*, p. 54.
6. Kumar, Dr. Ravindra, Sardar Vallabhbhai Patel and Com. Mao Tse Tung : A Comparative Study, p. 26.
7. Peasants struggle, p. 230.
8. *Ibid.*, p. 231.
9. Nehru, Pt. J.L., An Autobiography, New Delhi, 1982., p. 297.
10. Patel, Manubehn, V. Borsad Satyagraha, Navjivan, Ahmedabad, p. 37.
11. Kumar, Dr. Ravindra, Life and Work of Kanjibhai Desai, Surat, 1989, p. 159.
12. *Ibid.*, p. 17.
13. Prasad Dr. Rajendra, An Autobiography, Sastra Sahitya Mandal, New Delhi, 1962, p. 637.
14. Nehru, Pt. J.L., An Autobiography, New Delhi, 1982.
15. Home Political 1930, F. No. 25/30, National Archives of India, New Delhi.
16. Peasants struggle ....New Delhi, 1984, p. 302.
17. Home Department Political 1931, F. No. 33/31, National Archives of India, New Delhi.
18. Home Political 1930, F. No. 17/2/30 (I), P.A. Lucknow, U.P.
19. Home Political 1936, F. No. 4/8/36., National Archives of India, New Delhi.
20. "In the United Provinces there had been an acute economic crisis for some time past. In November 1930-32, Mr. H.N. Brailsford, the well known socialist writer, who was an altogether independent observer, told the writer in Calcutta that the conditions in the United Provinces were verging on an agrarian revolution. About this time the no-rent campaign was started by the Congress in the Province. After the Delhi truce, when the no-tax campaign was suspended, the peasants being in the same conditions as in 1930, could not pay their rent. In May, the Mahatma tried to mediate in the matter and advised the peasants to pay 50 per cent of their dues – but that also they could not. Thereupon the Government remitted a portion of the land revenue and maintained that was enough. The peasants thought otherwise and on their behalf, the provincial Congress committee tried to carry on negotiations with the government. In November matters reached a crisis. The Government demanded that the peasants should pay up their dues pending negotiations. The peasants demanded, on the contrary, that pending negotiation, the collection should be suspended. At this stage the provincial Congress committee approached Sardar Vallabhbhai Patel, the Congress president, and Mahatma Gandhi, who was then in Europe, for advice. The Mahatma Gandhi left it to the

committee to do as they thought best. The peasants' league (Kisan League) of the United Provinces then took the matter in hand and informed the Congress committee that if they did not start the no-rent compaign, it would be launched by the Kisan League. Faced with the possibility of losing its hold on the mass, the provincial Congress committee decided to commence the no-rent campaign. Immediately this was done, an ordinance was issued for suppressing the campaign. A large number of arrests was made under the ordinance and about the middle of December, when Pandit Jawahar Lal Nehru and Mr. Sherwani were leaving Allahabad for Bombay to make preparations for the reception of Mahatma they were arrested in the train." Indian Struggle, Subhas Chandra Bose.

21. Home Political 1931, F. No. 33/31, National Archives of India, New Delhi.
22. Patel, Sardar Vallabhbhai J., Speeches, edited by Parikh and Shah, Navjivan, Ahmedabad, 1949, p. 305.
23. Home Political 1931, F. No. 6/31, National Archives of India, New Delhi.
24. "One of the most significant features of the Lucknow Congress is the attention paid to the Agrarian Problem. This no doubt is due to the increasing influence of the socialist left wing and to the views of the president (Pandit Nehru), while the fact that somewhat half-hearted resolution have been passed and no very definite programme down up goes to show, the strength of the opposition on the right wing composed of landholders or persons with 'vested interest'. It would be unwise to over-estimate the strength of the opposition or to assume that very little will be done because of the division of Congress camp." – "Congress and the Agrarian Problem", Home Deptt. Political 1936, File No. 4/8/36, page No. 2, National Archives of India, New Delhi.
25. Home Political 1936, F. No. 4/7/36, National Archives of India, New Delhi.
26. Rao, Dr. V.K.R.V., The Nehru Legacy, p. 61.
27. *Ibid.*

# CHAPTER V

# Nehru and Kisan Leadership

Jawaharlal Nehru on local, provincial and national, three levels provided the leadership both in direct and indirect forms with the purpose of settling the direction of the peasantry for future and to solve its immediate problems. And with this purpose, rose the Oudh's Eka peasants struggle of 1920-21, the United Provinces' no-rent struggle of 1930-34 and the peasantry's struggle all over the country in 1939 and subsequent period. The existence of these struggles was confined not only upto one struggle and neither these struggles were the only part of the political movement but these yielded some certain results while solving the immediate problems and for the pleasureful economic development of the peasants in the time to come.

## The Oudh peasants struggle – The Eka movement – and Nehru's leadership

In the Gandhian era of national liberation movement the Eka peasants movement was the first well organised movement of the peasantry in Oudh region of then United Provinces and there was direct leadership of Jawaharlal Nehru to provide it with speed. The peasantry in spite of being the main class of the society as it had been unorganised in order to solve its problems, from that point of view the Oudh movement was unprecedented occurrence. There had been two major achievements of it in 1921-22.

(a) By that time the Oudh peasants had been in want of their self made organisation and in this regard by then their weakness transformed into their strength. The peasantry became influential, awakened and active class.

(b) Through this struggle the ideology which for the first time developed among the peasantry that was the heavy opposition of the foreign government's hegemony and active opposition of the rent and taxes. In spite of its staunch devotion to the religion the peasantry at that time had taken such steps which were supposed not to be retreated."[1]

As it is already mentioned in Chapter 1, Pandit Nehru had provided this movement with his direct leadership in June, 1920. Due to it there had also been an important feature of this movement that "namely known as Eka movement in United Provinces, it was fought on the economic and political basis perfectly. Though in various districts its main reason was the annoyance against exploitation by the landlords, yet it was the first organised peasants movement of the Gandhian era as it has been already mentioned. This struggle has attained glory in the Indian history of being the first organised one from the point of view of the peasant movements."[2] Except Pratapgarh, Rai Bareli and Allahabad districts this struggle was also sharp and "at several places it had dishonoured the British government while having challenged it openly. It can be said another important happening of it."[3] Though in Oudh the peasants also resorted to violence which was not fully in accordance with the principles of Nehru, yet "this struggle generated the stream of revolution among the peasants and villagers in some parts of northern India and western region. It was given the term of beginning of revolution in northern India in the British and some other newspapers of the east."[4]

It was a reality that this peasants struggle, locally commenced under the guidance and leadership of Nehru in Oudh region of United Provinces, had definitely generated a new stream of zeal and struggle all over the country. It will be analysed later. Here it is essential to clear that Nehru had derived considerable results through directing it. As it is known that in existence the chief basis of this movement was "to make an end of all the different kinds of exploitation by the landlords and re-assessment of land reforms and rent system and their limitation. And the peasants had become determined firmly for it."[5] Their preparedness and firm determination had also turned into violence and its zenith appeared on "February 4, 1922, in Chauri-chaura village of then Gorakhpur district of United Provinces (now of Deoria district of

Uttar Pradesh) where most of the peasants intruded the police station and set it on fire while chasing the policemen who had shot at them."[6] In today's background for us the easy imagination of it is not possible but it was a reality that then the better peasants organisation had transformed the political condition of the country."[7]

Soviet historians, while analysing the Oudh peasants movement led by Jawaharlal Nehru which had shown the way to the peasantry throughout the country, have accepted that "in the end of 1921, the political condition of India had become extremist. Its reason was the stepping up of the peasants movement towards extremism because the common man was getting strengthened from it."[8] This analysis is quite correct. Nehru has himself interpreted the peasantry, the Oudh Eka movement and its awakening and the consequences it yielded. It is also essential to know his interpretation before knowing its wonderful consequences due to his leadership of it.

As we know well that Nehru was directly linked with this movement. See his own words, "In 1921, I went continuously for the whole of the year in the countryside and my activities became rampant throughout the whole of Province."[9]

It resulted in the prevailing of provocation and maximum activeness in the countryside and the Congress activists turned towards the countryside or villages.[10] It was an unprecedented event and its yielding in of bigger result was also natural and as it is already stated that the peasants especially of Oudh region in spite of living in the peaceful atmosphere too became provoked. It did not mean that the peasants began violence from their side but they got prepared to defend themselves against violence and they became mightier to counter the violence through violence."[10A]

For them (the peasants) became difficult to bear the oppression and physical torturing by the Taluqdars, landlords and their guards, the policemen. And to face this difficulty the peasantry used its organisation. Due to it the peasants then took collective steps and their direct confrontation including the counter-violent activities were preplanned and full of wisdom. As :

(a) "The peasants used to go collectively by train even without tickets in the big public meetings especially which contained sixty or seventy thousands people and which usually used to take place after two or three months. Due to their collectivity the officials used to become helpless and they were unable to persecute them. The peasants used to say arrogantly and firmly that the olden days were over then."[11] All it was untolerable for the government and thus getting of the peasants organised was a challenge for it. It was the cause of beginning of confrontation.

(b) "The second major thing was that when the peasants did such type of activities, they used to do these most wisdomfully. And when they were prosecuted in the courts, they (the peasants) used to gherao (encircle) the courts heavily and by hook or crook they used to get released the peasant leaders."[12] On seeing this mobilization of the peasants not only the then United Provinces government but the governmenvt of India too became heavily worried and due to it in the end of 1921, in a government report of the United Provinces to the government of India, it was stated, "The peasants movement has entered the serious state and now it is necessary that their demands regarding the rent and land should be considered and in this connection the essential enactment should be done."[13] It was the helplessness of the government because the peasantry had become fearless and there was direct and valuable contribution of Nehru in order to make them (the peasants) undaunted.[14] For this contribution an instance is being given at reference number 14, which is in his own (Nehru's) words.

In this Oudh Eka Movement thousands of arrests were done, numerous persons died but the peasants had become undaunted and 'the government was forced to lessen the problems of the peasants through enactment in 1929.' This movement had the unique leadership of Nehru and the peasants faced the cases (suits) of the government, numerous persons died in prisons, numerous persons suffered sentences in prisons, numerous persons suffered hardships in the memory of their youth sons, brothers and friends but the peasants stepped ahead towards a certain direction. Its leader Jawaharlal Nehru was also sent to prison. Even then the most success which was received in this struggle was, in Nehru's words, "The major change through achievement of this movement was that the Oudh peasants formally got the right of life-long tenancy. Though it was not much improvement in the condition of the peasants, yet even after this partial success this peasants' commotion remained continued in its either minimum or maximum form by 1929."[15] Thus the peasants kept their struggle continued and they reached at the entrance of no-rent agitation of 1930.

*(b) Nehru and No-rent Satyagraha*

While analysing the nature and reality of Indian peasants Nehru has said, "Their strength of organisation did not stay for more period and developed in it the active mobilization did not last for long time."[16] It is also a historical fact because whenever the peasants collectively revolted against their oppression, it did not last for long time (or it could not be transformed into a protracted war of rebellion) but if the leadership again aroused consciousness of them, they again moved on the path of struggle. The same situation developed at the time of Civil disobedience movement in 1930, when Nehru in prison developed the idea of No-rent Movement and wisely got it implemented through the commencement of struggle or agitation."[17]

By the time of beginning the Salt Satyagraha, there was the presence of peasants activities. It is also a truth with this above-mentioned truth that the basis of these activities was prior- Oudh's and subsequent 'the Eka peasants movements of the whole of United Provinces led by Jawaharlal Nehru'. But in 1929, it had become motionless. Then on the eve of beginning of Salt Satyagraha the circumstances of United Provinces for peasants struggle were different. According to the writer of a history of Indian freedom struggle...."As it happened in Bardoli, the same way organised struggle was not there in United Provinces. Even then some time before the commencing of Salt Satyagraha or in 1929, and during the period of it fast peasants' activities had begun. Jawaharlal Nehru himself had participated in these activities."[18] After being released from prison he had spent his whole time for the peasants' activities.

In April 1930, soon Nehru was arrested as the Congress's President during the Salt Satyagraha and under arrest when he was in Naini prison, he thought to commence 'No-rent Struggle' of the peasants on provincial level. In the midst of the course of different events, "finally this struggle began and became fast but no so much fast as it had been in Oudh before." Began in November-December, 1930, this struggle had to rest after the placing of Gandhi-Irwin Pact when Nehru had personally appealed while visiting different places and at that time the peasants had become annoyed and due to their fastness of zeal they had become organised all over the province. It was an another occasion when the peasants struggle had yielded influential result.

During the period of 1931-33, the peasants movement of United Provinces yielded some concrete results. As :

(a) The first important work this No-rent Peasants Movement of United Provinces did that it inspired the peasants on national level. From its inspiration the organised peasants movements under the leadership of Kisan Sabha refused to pay taxes in Punjab, Bihar, Bengal, Karnatak and Andhra Pradesh. In Kashmir the peasants and their assistants, handicraftmen inclined towards struggle. The most dread result of the peasants revolt appeared in Alwar State of Rajputana where in the end of 1932, the rebel peasants, whose number was 30,000 and who were armed, had successfully encircled the several cities and villages of the northern part of the State and reached near Alwar city."[20]

(b) The second important result came of this struggle which was begun from the inspiration and leadership of Jawaharlal Nehru that the peasantry in addition to the British ruled areas became awakened and inclined to struggle even in the native states. It was certainly a step of success on the path of the country's freedom.[21]

(c) No-rent movement had spread almost all over the United Provinces and it had heavily reduced the powers of the landlord class, landowners and Taluqdars; even it abated their social value. Their reduced powers and social value could never be restored in spite of the fact that the British government had tried its best in their favour."[22]

(d) The landlords and their parallel persons used to physically torture the peasants but during the No-rent Movement such happenings were reduced continuously. Just reverse of it the peasants on getting the chance began to seize and assault the landlords. Simultaneously the money-lender class itself became lenient on seeing such happenings with the landlords."[23] In 1931, several landlords were stopped and wounded in the ways for they had punished the peasants in the past in Pratapgarh, Rai Bareli, Allahabad and other adjoining areas."[24] Though all these violent activities were against the will of Nehru, yet the importance of peasants' courage could not be minimised. There was a time when a correspondent of 'Leader' newspaper, while describing the pitiful narration of inhuman oppression of the peasants of Rai Bareli district, had written, "I have seen a large number of peasants of many villages. The narration of their hardships is really miserable. Numerous of them have been beaten mercilessly by the police even without the permission of District Police Superintendent. Numerous Taluqdars have taken law and order in their hands. Without any reason police have arrested 400 persons. The servants of Taluqdars have captured and detained numerous peasants."[25] After the No-rent Movement all these excesses were ceased which was a big success.

(e) 'The Congress began talks with the government in order to solve the peasants problems and appointed its a senior leader Govind Ballabh Pant to remain continuously in touch with the government.'[26] Or the Congress busied itself in solving the peasants problems because in a form the peasants had become the strong pillar of its strength.

## Nehru and the Peasants Movement of 1939

The peasants struggle which was begun from 1920-21 and 1922, in Oudh under the leadership of Jawaharlal Nehru that the Salt Satyagraha transformed fastly into the No-rent Movement throughout the whole of United Provinces and extended all over India. In 1939, the Second World War began and the provincial ministries of the Congress resigned. Consequently again the commotion of struggle began in the peasantry. And as the personal civil disobedience began, the common Congressmen especially those activists who had prior experience of the peasants struggles, became active and reached in midst of the peasants. Among them especially there were the Congress socialists who had been fully influenced from Nehru."[27] Though there was not direct leadership of Nehru for any peasants struggle at that time, yet inspiration from him was surely there. Due to it during the

Second World War once more again in India had stirred the peasants struggle fastly in United Provinces, Bihar, Bengal, Andhra and other provinces where there was the landlord system.'"[28] This struggle had not only provided the personal civil disobedience but the Quit India Movement too with heavy strength.

Thus, we studied, on three levels the leadership provided by Jawaharlal Nehru to the peasantry and found that under his direction in the peasantry took place many important and full of consciousness changed states or conditions. Among these following were the main :

(a) In the peasantry appeared, the might of getting organised collectively, the tendency of helping each other peasant in misery, the feeling of faith for collectively combating the opponent. This feeling remained into being in the peasantry by the time of getting independence which was long recollectable event in the history of Indian peasant struggles.

(b) In the peasantry appeared uniformity for the leadership which was another main transformative factor. In Oudh with which honesty and seriousness of conviction Nehru provided leadership to the peasantry, from it the peasants had fully become respectful for him. Nehru never hurt the sentiments of the peasants and again and again he showed his serious interest towards the peasants too.[29] Whether there is question of the time of Gandhi-Irwin Pact or of any day of subsequent period he always remained loyal for the peasants. In 1937, Nehru continuously emphasised for enactment in their favour in accordance with his promises for them and moreover had severely criticised those persons who used to think about the peasants unsympathetically.

Nehru's leadership to the peasants in an inspiring message even today for the peasant leaders who are honest, serious and reliable and who minutely watch the problems of the peasantry. This message tells us that we can imagine the miseries of others through suffering ourselves hardships and thus we can do work to eradicate these.

# References


1. Namboodripad, E.M.S., A History of Indian Freedom Struggle, Trivandrum 1986, p. 303.
2. *Ibid.*, p. 301.
3. *Ibid.*, pp. 302-3.
4. *Ibid.*, p. 33.
5. Home Political 1921, F.No. (B) 13/1921., National Archives of India, New Delhi.
6. Antonova K.A. and others, History of Indian Moscow, U.S.S.R., p. 561.
7. Namboodripad, E.M.S., A History of Indian Freedom Struggle, Trivandrum, 1986, p. 303.
8. Antonova K.A. and others, History of India, p. 560.
9. Right through the year 1921 I continued my visits to the rural areas, but my field of activities grew till it comprised the whole of the United Provinces. Non-Co-operation had begun in earnest and its message had reached the remotest village. A host of Congress workers in each district went about the rural areas with the new message to which they often added, rather vaguely, a removal of Kisan grievances. Swaraj was an all-embracing word to cover everything. Yet the two movements – Non-Co-operation and the Agrarian – were quite separate, though they overlapped and influence each other greatly in our province. As a result of Congress preaching litigation went down with a rush and villages established their Panchayats to deal with their disputes. Especially powerful was the influence of the Congress in favour of peace for the new creed of non-violence was stressed wherever the Congress worker went. This may not have been fully appreciated for understood but it did prevent the peasantry from taking to violence." – Nehru Pandit J.L. : An Autobiography, p. 58-9.
10. *Ibid.*

10-A. Kumar, Dr. Ravindra, Social and Political Ideas of Sardar Vallabhbhai J. Patel, Mittal Publications, New Delhi, 1990, p 270.

11. Home Political 1921, F.No. 10/21, National Archives of India, New Delhi.
12. *Ibid.*
13. Home Political 1921, F. No. 13/21, National Archives of India, New Delhi.
14. "I had just returned to Allahabad from Nagpur Congress when I received a telegram from Rae Bareli asking me to go there immediately as trouble was expected. I left the next day. I discovered that some leading Kisans had been arrested some days back and had been lodged in the local gaol. Remembering their success at Pratapgarh and the tactics they had then adopted, the peasants marched to Rae Bareli town for a mass demonstration. But this time the Government was not going to permit it and additional police and military had been collected to stop the Kisans. Just outside the town on the other side of a little river, the main

body of Kisans was stopped. Many of them, however, streamed in from other direction. On arrival at the Station I learnt of this situation and immediately I proceeded straight to river where the military were said to face the peasants. On the way I received a hurriedly written note from the District Magistrate asking me to go back. I wrote my reply on the back of it enquiring under what law and what section he was asking me to go back and till I heard from him I proposed to go on. As I reached the river sounds of firing could be heard from the other side. I was stopped at the bridge by the military and as I waited there I was suddenly surrounded by large numbers of frightened Kisans who had been hiding in the fields on this side of the river. So I held a meeting of about a couple of thousand peasants on the spot and tried to remove their fear and lessen their excitement. It was rather an unusual situation with firing going on their brethren within a stone's throw across a little stream and the military in evidence everywhere. But the meeting was quite successful and took away the edge from the Kisans' fear." – Nehru, Pt. J.L., An Autobiography, p. 62.

15. *Ibid.*
16. *Ibid.*
17. Kumar, Dr. Ravindra, Social and Political Ideas of Sardar Vallabhbhai J. Patel, p. 24.
18. Namboodiripad, E.M.S., A History of Indian Freedom Struggle, p. 458.
19. Home Political 1930-31, Files No. 11, 12/30, 1/31, National Archives of India, New Delhi.
20. Antonova K.A. and others, History of India, Moscow 1982, pp. 596-7.
21. *Ibid.*
22. Home Political 1935, 1 to 12 of 1935 (fortnightly reports) National Archives of India, New Delhi.
23. *Ibid.*
24. Home Political 1931, 32 and 33, Files of fortnightly Intelligence Reports, National Archives of India, New Delhi.
25. Young India, 26-1-1921, Edited by Mahatma Gandhi from Navjivan Press, Ahmedabad.
26. Home Political 1931, F. No. 3/31, National Archives of India, New Delhi.
27. Namboodiripad, E.M.S., A History of Indian Freedom Struggle, p. 555.
28. *Ibid.*, pp. 555-6.
29. Home Political 1931, F. No.-23/33/31, National Archives of India, New Delhi.

# CHAPTER VI

# Nehru and the Peasants Organisation

**(a) The Oudh Kisan Sabha**
**(b) The U.P. Kisan Sabha**
**(c) The All India Kisan Sabha**
**(d) Other Organisations of the peasantry**

Perhaps a few of today's political scientists, historians and the leaders working for the peasantry must by acquainted with this fact that Jawaharlal Nehru in the beginning of his public life had begun to perceive the miseries and hardships of the peasants and he had associated himself with the peasant organisations since the very beginning. Firstly he began from Allahabad district. Long before of the Non-Co-operation and Khilafat movement "the Congress Committee of Allahabad district, under the leadership of its president, Purushottam Das Tandon, had done important work for the amelioration of the peasantry. At that time Jawaharlal Nehru was in local politics as a member of the district Congress Committee."[1] In this form he too got associated with the peasants problems and their organisation but here it is too most essential to clear that he did not get suddenly or accidently linked with the peasants organisation. There was a certain background of maturing or of taking shape of his socialist ideology which inspired him to work for the emancipation of the most oppressed class – the peasantry in Indian society. While studying in Britain he had come into touch of socialist ideology and its thinkers. He had become serious due to being mentally equipped from this ideology which he had gained from the occurrence of the Soviet socialist revolution and the Indian circumstances or conditions and with it he was inspired to do the work for the amelioration of the peasants as they were excessively groaning under the yoke of slavery and poverty with the general conditions of Indian people's wretchedness. These circumstances were most wretched. According to a social scientist "During the First World War when Britain had laden its major military expenditure on the shoulders of its chief colony (India) at that time the excessive exploitation of this country yielded the grave consequences for the common people – the peasantry. Especially these consequences were destructive for the future of the peasants."

"Due to the consequenses of disorder of world economic relations during the war period the export of Jute, Cotton and Sesame-like technical crops suffered badly and it inflicted a heavy blow on the interests of the peasants. The landlord and moneylender class tried to recover its loss through accelerating the exploitation of the direct producers – the peasants. In between the period of 1911 to 1925, the debt of moneylenders upon the peasants had become double, of about 600 crores of rupees."

"In this exploitation the government had given full liberty to the landlords, landowners and moneylenders to commit every oppression on the peasants. The datum of 600 crores of rupees which is mentioned above, that was merely on the basis of government indications but the reality was more reverse of it."

"The government, its agents – the moneylenders, its intermediaries – the Taluqdars, landlords and landowners having taken back the land in large quantity from the peasants began to let it for more rent in the cases where the peasants were merely the temporary and just *ad hoc* tenants. Where there was the other situation of the peasants or where the peasants were not tenants, where directly the peasants through the medium of Patels and Patwaris used to give rent to the government, there the peasants against their debts or loans had to mortgage their lands with the moneylenders and thus, they lost their lands. The preceding situation was mainly of the United Provinces and the other situation was mostly of the Punjab."

"The victims of the government's and its native or indigenous agents' repression were not only the peasants but all the other villager toiling people too as carpenters, ironsmiths, weavers, washermen and labourers. Finally from all of them the agriculture sector was to be affected because all they were dependent on the peasants for their livelihood. Thus, on the one hand the peasants went towards destruction and on the other the village handicraft was fully ruined."

"The next bad affect on the peasants was that in spite of doing hard labour they were unable to fill their stomachs due to the soaring prices of essential commodities. The want of edible articles and soaring prices of these not only affected the peasantry or the common countryside people but the urban middle class persons, intellectuals and white collar workers too. Even then finally and mostly the toiling people of the countryside including the peasants and others were affected."

"The national bourgeoisie of India who had expanded its enterprises during the war period and who had strengthened its economic condition then became more vigilant or cautious towards the bans caused by colonial oppression and the coming consequences of the partiality oriented steps taken by the colonial officials in the different fields of the country's economic, political and cultural matters. This class (national bourgeoisie) was willing its economic progress. So its target of exploitation were also the lower classes including the peasantry and the other toiling people because it was out of its capacity to influence the British government and its economic interests."

"In the beginning of third decade of twentieth century the condition of India had become of different kind. At that time two sharp contradictions were prevailing in the society of India. A contradiction was there between the indigenous exploiting classes and the native exploited classes. The other contradiction was there between the Indian indigenous exploiting classes and the British imperialists or the foreign exploiters. Then the British imperialists were trying to win over the endorsement of Indian exploiting classes including the feudal landowners, kings and comprador bourgeoisie and their indigenous accomplices the traders and moneylenders."

"The fastness in the National emancipation struggle came with the appearing of zeal's wave among the workers and villager peasants. In 1918, in Bombay, Madras, Kanpur and Ahamedabad occurred unprecedented workers struggles due to the country's then political and economic circumstances. These workers struggles were based on that time's economic condition of them which was most miserable because after the First World War as the deterioration came in economic field, innumerable workers had become unemployed. Then the workers' economic condition was quite similar of the peasants'."[2]

Nehru came back from Britain to his natal country and here whatever he found through personally and practically seeing, it was that with the economic loss of the First World War the whole of weight the imperialist government had placed on the Indian peasants and it had even gambled the existence of their lives."[3] It was the cause that on joining the local politics he immediately took interest in the peasants organisation. And subsequently this interest of him increased day by day. He himself has accepted that he was effected from the peasants who under those circumstances were the victims of exploitation and consequently his struggling for them. He has also accepted the most wretched condition of the peasantry.[4] And to get sanctioned justice for them was the most important requirement not only for the welfare of the peasants but to strengthen the economic system of the society, to brighten the country's future and to honour the vast public opinion as the peasants represented the majority of the people. So, Nehru immediately got himself linked with Oudh Kisan Sabha. In his autobiography Jawaharlal Nehru while describing about the peasantry has approved it himself in his own words and he has said that the condition of the peasants was so miserable that they used to look only with hopeful sights at any outsider person who came nearer of them. On seeing their standard of living and economic condition one was bound only to bend of shame. To remain hungry and to suffer from physical torturing by the landowners, landlords, money-lenders and police had become their daily routine. On the one hand the peasants had to do hard labour under warmth, sunshine and coldness, on the other hand they had to suffer of flogging, hunger and thirst.

## Nehru and the Oudh Kisan Sabha

As in the first chapter's portion of Nehru's link with the Oudh peasantry we have found it that how he got associated with the peasants and how he himself fought for the solution of their problems. On getting associated with the Oudh peasantry he mainly contributed two things for the peasants from his immortal thinking. These were following :

(a) Strengthening and mobilisation of the Organisation.

(b) Expansion of the Organisation.

### Strengthening and mobilisation of the organisation

On getting associated with the peasants organisation Nehru endeavoured excessively for strengthening and mobilisation of Kisan Sabha. Strengthening and mobilisation are complementary to each other. He was of the opinion that ...."If the peasants do not get fully organised, how they will overthrow the chronic tendency of exploitation of a certain class of handful persons – the exploiting class which is protected by the mightiest government of the world." So, the most essential thing for the peasants is the organisation, unorganised peasants will remain victims of oppression. He expressed the view that if the peasants in large number would not come in the organisation, it would be rather impossible to move even a step forward. He opined, "Without organisation the force only of number is useless. When the feeble threads of cotton are disunited, these are so weaker that these can be easily flown by even a slight puff of air and these can be divided into pieces but when in large number these are accumulated mutually and amicably and thus, when these are interwoven, these develop in the form of cloth, then their strength, beauty and utility are enhanced amazingly. When the peasants will be mutually united like the threads of cotton, they will come to know the importance of the organised strength. Disunited peasants have always been oppressed and thus, in the future will remain the same. So, if the peasants want their welfare, they will have to prepare their active and vigilant organisation in order to make themselves stronger and to take action. It will depend mostly on the feeling of mutual affection and trust for each other."[5]

A senior national leader* having picturised the reality of the peasants of United Provinces said : "For the peasant inhabitants of lacs of villages who are suffering of numerous diseases there is no medical aid arrangement. Shivering of the extreme coldness

* Sardar Vallabhbhai Patel

these peasants and their assistants have no proper cloths to put on and to bed. Their homes and huts are so rough and uneven that these are not worth of living for human beings. There are visible dunghills causing dirtness and badsmell all around the villages. Their age is diminishing. They are under the debt of crores of rupees. There is no way out for them to rescue. After facing coldness, warmth and rains and after doing hard labour for months the grain they produce, it is confiscated by the parasites or the exploiters even before its coming in the homes of the peasants. Whether there is sufficient production or not, whether the crop has been victim of drought or of extreme rain or of frost or of locusts or of down prices but the peasant has to pay rent compulsorily. The burden of recovery of the money not paid yet always remains on his head. Except it the moneylender keeps his eyes on the crop in order to recover his money of loan and its interest. Thus the peasants and their children suffer of hunger and their production of grain disappears even before coming in their homes. To prove this wretched condition of the peasants, it is not necessary to produce proofs and data."[6]

## The Oudh Kisan Sabha, Nehru and expansion of the organisation

When Nehru had associated himself with the Oudh Kisan Sabha at that time the peasants organisation from the point of view of strength and mobility it was only in Allahabad district. When he immediately took interest then mobilisation appeared in the neighbouring Pratapgarh district. Its reason was as it was also accepted by the then Government that Pratapgarh was adjacent to Allahabad district and then Allahabad city was a centre of political leaders and activities. If there was any atrocity or excess in any village it was just informed at Allahabad and therefrom just the necessary help and leadership were extended."[7] Nehru's steps continuously went ahead and the Kisan Sabha from Allahabad and Pratapgarh extended to the Faizabad, Sultanpur, Rai Bareli and Lucknow etc. After it the Kisan Sabha became active in Oudh. At that time in January, 1921, "The peasants of Rai Bareli had gallantly struggled against the oppression by the landlords and the government and its agent class."[8] Nehru for the expansion of the organisation had travelled the whole of Oudh on foot even without caring the season and thus, he had provided the peasants with courage. Sometimes Pandit Madan Mohan Malviya also accompanied him.

### Nehru, the Oudh Kisan Sabha, the Eka Movement and its consequenses

As it has been described in Chapter V, that in 1920-21, the Eka peasants movement under the leadership of Jawaharlal Nehru in Oudh region had taken place. This movement was stirred under the leadership of Kisan Sabha organisation and its consequenses had come ten years after in the form of fierce No-rent Struggle. But at that time as the Kisan Sabha had directed the peasants in a certain discipline and unity, its another example is not available in the whole of the history of peasants movement. Though this discipline did not stay in the peasantry for long "because by nature the peasantry cannot stay more in a certain state (situation) and soon it becomes out of control."[9] Even then the way to go forward at that time which was shown by Nehru and the Kisan Sabha to the peasants, it went of expanding day by day.

### The United Provinces Kisan Sabha and Nehru

In 1929, or in the year when under the presidentship of Nehru the most important and historical session of the Indian National Congress held at Lahore, the same year in the countryside of United Provinces the formation of strong units of the Kisan Sabha had been started. Simultaneously the reorganisation of old units of the Kisan Sabha began. This work remained continued in 1930."[10] Though at that time Nehru was the president of Indian National Congress, yet more than it he was fully conscious about the Kisan Sabha of United Provinces and he remained in constant touch with it as it is evident from the subsequent events which occurred in the last month of 1930.

Due to Nehru's special interest the Kisan Sabha came in the existence in every district of United Provinces of Agra and Oudh."[11] And there was unit of Kisan Sabha in every district. On the provincial level in accordance with the policy of the Congress then provincial president of the Congress committee, Tasadduq Ahmed Khan Sherwani, a big landlord was also the president of Kisan Sabha. Nehru was only a member of the provincial committee of it but it had a certain peculiarity that in spite of its president coming from landlord class the Kisan Sabha work progressed due to his (Nehru's) efforts, interest and inspiration. The great achievement of the Kisan Sabha of United Provinces under the leadership of Nehru was its decisive role in the establishment of All India Kisan Sabha and to turn the Congress wholly towards the peasants' problems otherwise the peasants would have taken indefinitely long time to come over their oppression as it is also shown in reference number twelve.[12]

It was definitely a miracle of the Kisan Sabha of United Provinces under the leadership of Nehru that only in March-April, 1932, 19717 persons went in jails of the Britishers in order to get sanctioned their rights.[13] For the whole of the details the arrangement is at next page's Chart No. 1.[14] It is also essential here to clear that these arrested persons were afraid of neither going to prison nor of tyranny of the landlords and the government. From the government record of Barabanki district alone of that time which is shown in Chart No. 2, we can imagine this fact.[15] Its other peculiarity was that under the leadership of Nehru the Kisan Sabha of United Provinces had prepared both at local and provincial levels such a strong force of vigilant, honest and dedicated activists like as it had come into being in 1928, during the Bardoli peasants movement in Gujarat.

In this strong force of United Provinces the main individuals were Shyamlal Nehru, Uma Nehru, Luxmi Chand Vakil, Mohanlal Saxena and Krishnakant Malviya. All these individuals, who came from middle class society, dedicated themselves for the cause of the peasants. These individuals had done unprecedented work especially in eastern U.P. under the leadership of Kisan Sabha from 1931 to 1933. These leading individuals were doing the work getting themselves away from the peasants cell of the provincial Congress committee and they were the symbols and defenders of the separate existence of the peasants organisation. They were shielded and directed by Nehru.

In the background of Nehru the strengthening and expansion of the organisation of Kisan Sabha has already been discussed sufficiently and it was actually the consequence of this policy that under the leadership of Kisan Sabha he himself commenced No-rent struggle in the province in 1930-33. It was the strong

## CHART NO. 1

During March and April, 1932, the persons who were arrested due to participating in the No-rent struggle led by the Kisan Sabha of United Provinces and were the villagers :

| Year | Month | Total number of the arrested persons | Male | Female |
|---|---|---|---|---|
| 1932 | March-April | 15230 | 14545 | 685 |
| | | | 18 | |
| | Growth in April | – It is datum of the persons arrested under ordinary laws. | | |
| 1932 | March-April | 905 | 883 | 22 |
| | | – These persons were arrested under special law. | | |
| 1932 | March-April | 1842 | 1823 | 19 |
| | | – The persons arrested under Arms Act. | | |
| 1932 | March-April | 1722 | 1586 | 186 |
| | | – The persons arrested under Section 718 of Crime Act. | | |
| 1932 | March-April | 118 | 117 | 1 |
| | | – The persons arrested under the new Ordinance promulgated in 1932. | | |
| | Total | 19717 | 18954 | 913 |

feeling of trust arose in the peasantry for Nehru which strengthened and mobilised the Kisan Sabha of United Provinces and it left out special marks on the peasants all over the country. Because Nehru was firm of action and promise regarding the affairs of the peasantry and the trust the peasants had on him, he did not wish to break it at any cost whether he had to face numerous difficulties. To prove this trust numerous examples can be cited but only one will suffice here. According to the provisions of Gandhi-Irwin Pact, the Salt Satyagraha was stopped and in the United Provinces on the appeal of Gandhiji and Nehru the peasants had ceased the no-rent struggle. After it in August-September Gandhiji went to London to participate in the Second Round Table Conference. Among the proposals which Gandhiji took with him, one of these was also regarding the problems of peasants. At the time of adjournment of no-rent struggle Nehru had assured the peasants that if the atrocities would be committed and the government and its agents would not abide by their promise of adjourning the recovery of rent, it would not be paid and the struggle again would be commenced."[18] But in the beginning of October month the oppression was again committed by the side of landlords and the government. Nehru had recollected his promise. He really arranged the green flag shown by the Kisan Sabha to the struggle. In this regard a telegram "on 16th October, 1931, was also sent to the Kingsway Hall, London."[19] This beginning, with the permission of the Congress's president, Vallabhbhai Patel, reached Allahabad, the home district of Jawaharlal Nehru. It is also mentioned as possibility in that telegram. The purpose of saying is that Nehru saw miseries of the peasants for years. He too saw confiscation and attaching of the goods of peasants and from all that he had become so harassed that he aimed at eradicating these unbearable miseries. "After all, how far the humanity will remain subject of the British oppression." It was the question with Nehru and the consequence of his search for the solution of it was the organised Kisan Sabha of United Provinces. Its enlargement was the All India Kisan Sabha.

## CHART NO. 2

List of the arrested persons and the cases filed against the rural persons in four Tehsils of Barabanki district from 1 to 7 July, 1931.

| | Name of Tehsil | No. of cases | Arrests |
|---|---|---|---|
| 1. | Nawabganj | 26 | 123 |
| 2. | Fatehpur | 43 | 100 |
| 3. | Ramsnehighat | 27 | 144 |
| 4. | Haidergarh | 5 | 6 |
| | Total | 101 | 373 |

In the chart shown above total 123 persons who were arrested in Nawabganj Tehsil, out of them 96 persons were arrested by the government on the complaints of landlords and their equivalents and the rest were rounded up by the police directly. Among these even three persons were sent to prison on their personal bonds. 152 persons were such who did not receive summons even. The same way in Fatehpur Tehsil 12 persons were arrested due to complaints and the rest were rounded up by the police and 115 did not receive summonses. In Ramsnehighat 70 persons were arrested due to complaints and the rest were rounded directly by the police. There 61 villagers did not receive summonses and the four persons had to furnish their personal securities. In Haidergarh Tehsil there were 38 such persons who did not receive summonses.[16] Out of total arrests, "167 arrests were there under section 124 and 25 villagers were there who were punished rigorously for serious offences."[17]

## Nehru and the All India Kisan Sabha

Even in 1934-35 or after the end of Civil disobedience movement the peasantry kept its struggle continued through the Kisan Sabhas throughout the country with the demand of abatement of rent at local, district and provincial levels. This struggle included the meetings, conferencess, and processions at village, tehsil headquarter and district levels.'[20] Then the spark of struggle of United Provinces had spread all over the country especially in Bihar, Punjab, Madras, Andhra etc. provinces and 'there the Kisan Sabhas had come into being not only at district levels but at the provincial levels too.'[21] Nehru had intensely visited Bihar, Bengal, Orissa, Bombay, Madras and Central Provinces and "during these visits the peasants organisation and their problems was the main theme of his speeches."[22]

Under these circumstance a separate and countrywide orgnisation of the Kisan Sabha was an essential task. With this purpose "in April, 1936, with the Congress conference at Lucknow, simultaneously held the first conference of All India Kisan Sabha".[23] Pandit Nehru was the President of this conference and he left no stone unturned to make the peasants organisation stronger.

## The Object and Programme of Kisan Sabha

After formation of the All India Kisan Sabha, its national council's plenum held in August, 1936. In it regarding the peasants, its object and programme was accepted :

"(a) Abolition of the landlord system.

(b) Reformation in the system of land revenue in Raiyyatvadi areas.

(c) Reduction in rent

(d) To Sharpen the peasants struggle etc."[24]

In this programme declared by the menifesto it was evident that with it the Kisan Sabha would accept heartily the national liberation movement. Later on this Kisan Sabha expanded sufficiently and Bihar's famous peasants leader and revolutionary Swami Sahajanand Sarswati, Andhra's N.G. Ranga, Gujrat's Indulal Yagnik etc. were its foremost leaders.

From 1937, the Kisan Sabha gained more momentum. "At that time the main form of the Kisan Sabha's activities was the mass propaganda. During this its workers, used to define policies to the masses of peasantry, tried to broaden its mass base and collected the signatures of the peasants for the applications of land reforms to be served to the representatives of the Congress's provincial governments."[25]

During the period of 1937-38, especially in "United Provinces, Bihar, Andhra and some other parts of the country in almost all the districts, where the units of All India Kisan Sabha were active, large processions and public meetings of the peasants were organised."[26] It was amazing that the Kisan Sabha which was founded in 1936, "its members' number in 1938, was 6 and half lacs and in 1939, before the beginning of Second World War it was 9 lacs."[27]

Thus, the All India Kisan Sabha, which was formed through the important step and effort of Nehru, getting the peasants organised it opened the way for them to get justice.

## Jawaharlal Nehru and the Bharat Krishak Samaj

Nehru throughout his whole of life endeavoured ceaselessly to make the peasants self-reliant, to get them emancipated from exploitation and to get sanctioned for them the honourable status in society and in this work he remained step by step successful. At last, the freedom came and the landlord system was abolished. In the Constituent Assembly on the question of land acquisition Nehru was just on a side. For the land reforms the ninth schedule was included in the constitution due to his efforts. In spite of all that Nehru knew that the peasants would take still more time to become self-reliant. Due to this reason "in 1950, in conformity with the will of Nehru a non-political insitution was founded. The name of this institution is the Bharat Krishak Samaj."[28]

The purpose of the Bharat Krishak Samaj is to improve consciousness of the peasants gradually regarding the growth of production through modern means and simultaneously to cooperate the government's every creative policy regarding the agriculture. It contributes even to solve the problems. "This institution has been in the foremost role of developing the modern agriculture through scientific methods and it has been excessively helpful to bring about green revolution."[28A]

Thus, after the explanation of the whole of chapter seriously we come to the numerous important conclusions of Nehru's relation with the organisation. These conclusions are about the organising capacity of that great personality, his organising ability and his organisational achievements through his organising ability.

The Oudh Kisan Sabha of his age was an indicative of Nehru's immortal message to the youths who came from upper and middle classes and who understood their certain duties for real India but even today it is a source of inspiration to the builders of independent India and leaders and thinkers who really think over the politics and society. Even today there is necessity of true organisations of that type, knowing the exact problems of the peasants and countryside India, doing the work for the solution of the problems and coordinating simultaneously the peasantry and its cooperators.

The same way the second big achievement of Nehru was to provide the Kisan Sabha of United Provinces with leadership. An arm of this achievement was the creation of permanent feeling of trust for him among the peasants and the other arm was to make the peasants attracted towards his organising capacity. In spite of getting educated from Cambridge and Harward universities and coming from a super class family as he created trust for him in the peasants and as he provided the peasants with courage to fight imperialism and the landlords, its another instance would not be available.

The All India Kisan Sabha was a symbol of understanding the hardships of the country's common people and the Bharat Krishak Samaj was indicative of the continuous progress of the peasants in post-independence India. As Nehru through these peasant organisations struggled for the welfare of the peasants and as he proved his ability, wisdom and fighting nature, in these qualities the seriousness and honesty which were inherent, these are mightier enough today to provide the peasant leaders with lesson in the independent country.

## References

1. Nehru, Pt. J.L., An Autobiography, New Delhi, 1986, p. 402.
2. Antonova, K.A. and others, History of India, Moscow.
3. Kumar, Dr. Ravindra, Life and Work of Kanjibhai Desai, Surat, 1989, p. 19.
4. Quoted from the Autobiography of Pt. Jawaharlal Nehru.
5. Kumar, Dr. Ravindra, Sardar Vallabhbhai Patel and Com. Mao Tse-Tung: A Comparative Study, 1988, p. 29.
6. *Ibid.*, p. 30.
7. Home Department Political, 1921, F. No. 13, National Archives of India, New Delhi.
8. Young India, Ahmedabad, January 26, 1921, edited by Mahatma Gandhi from Navjivan Press, Ahmedabad, p. 8.
9. Kumar, Dr. Ravindra, Sardar Vallabhbhai Patel and Com, Mao Tse-Tung; A Comparative Study, 1988, quoted from introduction.
10. Antonova, K.A. and others, History of India, Moscow, pp. 592-93.
11. Home Department Political, 1933, F. No. 13/16 and K.W. National Archives of India, New Delhi.
12. 'In the rule where the lazy traders, having upto Rupees one thousand income annually who even cause loss to the country instead of profit through running the shops of bidi, tobacco, foreign cloths or the teahotels, have not to pay any tax but the peasants who produce the wealth through doing hard labour over day and night and upon whose production depend State and the people, whether in their field there is production of crop or not, whether their children get the bread or not, even then they have surely to pay rent. If they do not pay it, their right upon their fields is snatched, their goods are confiscated and sold and they are imprisoned. What can be the benefit of showing mad anger or

of weeping against such direct and extreme injustice? Nothing. We have to fight these injustices. We have to attain our right and to get it we should unleash our heavy efforts. These efforts can take us towards success.' — Kumar, Dr. Ravindra, Sardar Vallabhbhai Patel and Com. Mao Tse-Tung: A Comparative Study, p. 29.

13. Home Department Political, 1933, F. No. 33/24, National Archives of India, New Delhi.
14. Home Department Political, 1933, F. No. 33/24, National Archives of India, New Delhi.
15. *Ibid.*
16. *Ibid.*
17. *Ibid.*
18. Home Department Political, 1931, F. No. 33/10/31, National Archives of India, New Delhi.
19. "Agrarian situation becoming critical. Coercive process, attachments, forcible collection rent continued right through without interval. Many ejected tenants proceeded against for criminal trespass, many for fear of permanently losing land sold cattle belongings borrowed money paid full demand plus extras. Fresh demand now made, for current season inadequate remissions threat that if full payment not made within month remission might be cancelled, also no objection considered on behalf of tenants till full payment made. Condition of Kisans deplorable, thoroughly exhausted after past six months continuous harassment by forcible measures, apparently process likely be repeated this season also. Allahabad district Congress Committee resolved under circumstances to ask permission to start satyagraha if necessity arises by advising withholding payment of rent, application for permission made to Vallabhbhai and provincial committee. Representative district Kisan Conference being held next week to decide question. Decision likely have for reaching consequenses but question about payment or withholding payment must be decided soon. Vital urgent problem for Kisans admitting no delay." — Home Deptt. Political 1931, Oct. No. D. 33/27/31.
20. Antonova, K.A. and others, History of India, Moscow, 1982, p. 607.
21. *Ibid.*, pp. 607 8.
22. Home Department Political, 1936, F. No. 4/38/36, 4/7/36 and 14/13/36 etc., National Archives of India, New Delhi.
23. Majumdar, R.C., History of Freedom Movement in India, Calcutta, 1962, p. 139.
24. Antonova, K.A. and others, History of India, p. 615.
25. *Ibid.*
26. Namboodiripad, E.M.S., A History of Indian Freedom Struggle, 1986, p. 475.
27. Antonova, K.A. and others, History of India, Moscow, 1982, pp. 616-7.
28. Peasants' struggles.

28-.A. *Ibid.*

## CHAPTER VII

# The Peasantry and the Congress Ministries
# Land Committee : Pant Report: Land Act

Due to the great struggle done by it on two fronts from 1920 to 1935, finally in 1937, the Indian National Congress 'on getting majority in seven provincial legislative assemblies out of eleven ones throughout India under the Government of India Act of 1935, got an opportunity of forming the government'.[1] One of these two fronts on which the Congress struggled was also the peasants movement stirred and led by Nehru and other leading unique leaders. So, it was most important that after taking over the power what point of view the Congress and its ministries adopted towards the peasants who had not cared for their lives even for the sake of the country's freedom. Though the opportunity, which the Congress had got to form the provincial governments, was not the full state of independence, yet Nehru and other leaders were fully sincere to the promises they had made for the peasants. Due to it after the elections when at Wardha the meeting of working committee of the Congress held, in it the seven points resolution which was accepted, its seventh point was regarding the peasants and other villagers.[2] According to these points the Congress ministries had to do the work. In this point (the seventh one) it was clear that whatever would be possible the peasants would be helped to solve their problem of rent and land revenue through liberal policies and cooperation.

The Congress even cleared it that the menifesto regarding primary demands of the peasants' problems which was produced at the time of Faizpur conference in 1936, every effort ought to be done to implement that. It was very important alternative resolution produced in the conference about the rights of the peasants. According to that resolution an imagination was formulated for 'expanding the peasants movement under the auspices of the Congress for the abatement of rent, moneylender's debt interest and land revenue. Its approval by the Congress (in the background of Kisan Sabha) was really something important and most fortunate'.[3]

The period from 1936 to 1938, was very important from the point of view of series of events of struggle of Indian peasants movement. There were two reasons of it. First of it was that the peasants struggle had gone ahead with the mighty speed. Hardly a year had passed since the formation of All India Kisan Sabha in 1936, that in provinces the Congress governments were formed. The formation of these Congress governments was the second important event. In these governments "numerous such persons by inherence had entered who were chiefly dedicated for the peasants' deeds even while remaining in the Congress. They were well acquainted with the problems of peasants and already they had struggled for the solution of these. Nehru himself was the chief of the Congress organisation. Already he had been struggling severely for the last seventeen years for the cause of peasants. Sardar Vallabhbhai Patel was the chief of the Parliamentary committee to guide the Congress governments. He had already led the peasants in Kaira, Borsad and Bardoli. Their equivalent was the Chief Minister of United Provinces, Mr. Govind Ballabh Pant who was well acquainted with the peasants' problems."[4] At the same time the newly formed Congress Governments were worried for the peasants and some of these had begun to take steps regarding the abatement of rent etc. in conformity with the resolution passed in the Faizpur conference.

## Land Committee and the Pant Report

Then the steps which were being taken by the government, these were based on the Pant Report. In 1931, after the Gandhi-Irwin pact when the civil disobedience movement and the no-rent struggle were adjourned, at that time the question of peasants' problems was main. At that time it was essential to have a talk with the government on the general problems of the peasants as rent, tenancy and occupant tenancy etc. With this purpose "the Congress committee of United Provinces deputed its a senior leader Govind Ballabh Pant to remain in touch with the government."[5] The economic conditions were highly miserable at that time in 1931. Deterioration in agriculture field, excessively down prices and unability of the peasants to pay rent in accordance with the demand were the chief symptoms of that time's Indian society."[6] Then the question with the government was that what, how much and in which form the assistance could be given to the peasants. Before it the government had been only consulting the landowners and never the peasants in such matters. But the landowners never agreed on any such condition by which instead of the government their own economic interests were to be harmed. And thus, any assistance to their peasants in the form of reduction in rent the landowners had never been giving.

When the no-rent struggle stopped, the Congress, Gandhiji and Nehru appealed the peasants to pay rent but as it is mentioned above that there was deterioration in the agriculture field. So, the representatives of "the peasants demanded heavy abatement of rent which was not conceded by the government in practice for a long time. Its reason was the absence of then Governor, Sir Malcolm Helley."[7] But the government's action was essential in this regard immediately from the special point of view of implementing the provision of Pact. Even then the acting Governor delayed it in the absence of the Governor, Helley and thus, the condition of peasants remained miserable seriously.

Then the month of October came. That was the time when the second crop instalment of rent was to be realized. Due to this seriousness the provincial government appointed a small committee. In this committee there were some officials of the government and some local landlords. In it there was no representation of the peasants. Of course when this government committee began to function formally, the government asked Govind Ballabh Pant to become a member of it but Pant did not accept it because of the last moment of it and minding the dignity of being the Congress's representative and moreover by that time it had already taken several important decisions."[8]

As an alternative of the government committee, the U.P. Congress Committee appointed a separate committee regarding rent and land. This small committee was formed in order to collect the facts and details of past and present about agriculture and to submit its report soon. There were three members of this committee namely Mr. Rafi Ahmad Kidwai, Venkatesh Narayan Tiwari and the president, Govind Ballabh Pant. "This committee submitted a lengthy report (popularly known as the Pant report) in which there were details with data regarding agriculture of United Provinces, agriculture conditions and the points of relief for the peasants."[9]

According to the provisions of Gandhi-Irwin Pact the government had said "to realize rent 50% from common peasants and by 75% from other peasants but Gandhiji had not agreed with it and he had been insisting on price-crop-rent formula to make the basis of realization."[10] The Pant Report accepted the statement of Gandhiji to be genuine. Simultaneously the village labourer's wage and cost of production were too made clear.

As it has already been mentioned that the Congress governments in provinces which were formed in 1937, these then began to take legislative steps regarding the peasants. "In the first round the Congress governments in several provinces appointed committees to suggest that how the legal proceeding could be done to assist the peasants and how the conditions of rent and land could be made liberal in accordance with the Pant Report."[11] It was also a subject "under consideration that what steps could be taken to abolish the landlord and landowner systems."[12]

The Congress governments went on unleashing their efforts and "the then Bombay government took two important steps. The first step was to liberalise the landlord system and to make permanent the occupant tenant peasants and to enhance their rights."[13] The second step of the Bombay government was that legally it gave back the lands of those peasants whose lands were confiscated while struggling against the government and the landlord system."[14] It was most important and historical decision. The same way to bring about a turn in the landlord system and to sanction more rights to the peasants on the basis of the peasant and the landlord agreement the Congress Government of Bihar through legislation abolished the Bhawali system which had been strangling the throats of the peasants."[15] The similar steps were taken in United Provinces and other provinces.

When in the presence of the Congress ministries the first big conference of the Congress held at Haripura in 1937, in it a resolution was passed as it is mentioned in reference No. 16. The Congress governments got an opportunity to do work for very short period. Though there were in the Congress ministries the supporters of landlords, yet these did maximum work whatever could be possible in spite of their limited powers. These Congress ministries, as it is well known, at the beginning of Second World War had resigned their offices and these could not enact on the basis of recommendations of the appointed committees." It was their bad luck or bad circumstance but whatever these did that was surely pleasureful performance regarding change. The series of this change yielded the beginning of abolition of landlord system.

Thus, through studying the mutual relation between the Congress ministries and the peasantry we come to the conclusion that in this field the Congress party at that time played an important role. This role was indicative of the political and economic transitions in future and Nehru contributed a lot for these decisions to be taken behind this role. He was an advocate of the natural and fundamental rights to be given to the people. His ideology was crystal clear. He had understood the importance of agriculture and the peasantry in their true form and to highlight this importance he had been always desirous of to enact in this regard appropriately. The reckoning of importance of agriculture and the peasants by him is quite evident from his statement : "My full emphasis may be for industries, my full force may be for steel plants but I firmly say that the agriculture is more important than all these or any industry."

'The right of land (possessing) can only be of its tiller and producer of wealth from it, the peasant. With this fact Nehru had always been associated and he never disassociated himself from it under all the circumstances whether that was the occasion of Gandhi-Irwin Pact or that of functioning of the Congress Ministries in 1937. The praise of his efforts can be done through well seeing the improved future of the peasants.

## References

1. Tendulkar, D.G., The Mahatma, Volume 5, p. 213.
2. "Congress members should press for the carrying out of the Congress programme as enunciated in the election manifesto and the Congress agrarian resolution. In particular, they should work for –
   - (i) a substantial reduction in rent and revenue,
   - (ii) assessment of income-tax, on a progressive scale, on agricultural incomes, subject to a prescribed minimum,
   - (iii) fixity of tenure,
   - (iv) relief from the burden of rural debt and arrears of rent and revenue,
   - (v) repeal of all repressive laws,
   - (vi) release of political prisoners, internees and detenues,
   - (vii) restoration of lands and property confiscated or sold by government during civil disobedience movement,
   - (viii) eight hours day for industrial workers, without reduction of pay, living wage,
   - (ix) prohibition of intoxicating liquor and drugs,
   - (x) unemployment relief, and
   - (xi) reduction of high salaries, allowances, and cost of administration of government." – Namboodripad, E.M.S., A History of Indian Freedom Struggle, pp. 627-8.
3. Antonova, K.A. and others, History of India, Moscow 1982, p. 613.
4. Kumar, Dr. Ravindra, Social and Political Ideas of Sardar Vallabhbhai J. Patel, Mittal Publication, New Delhi, 1990, p. 172.
5. Nehru, Pt. Jawaharlal, An Autobiography, 1988, p. 264.
6. Tendulkar, D.G., The Mahatama, Volume III, Publication Division, New Delhi, p. 36.
7. Antonova, K.A. and others, History of India, Moscow, p. 623.
8. Nehru, Pandit Jawaharlal, An Autobiography, 1988, p. 307.
9. *Ibid.*
10. Tendulkar, D.G., The Mahatma, Volume III, New Delhi, p. 47.
11. Guha, A.C., India's Struggle Quarter of a Century, Publication Division 1982, p. 313.
12. *Ibid.*
13. Kumar, Dr. Ravindra, Life and Work of Kanjibhai Desai, Surat, 1989, p. 142.
14. Kumar, Dr. Ravindra, Sardar Vallabhbhai Patel and Com. Mao-Tse Tung: A Comparative Study, Muzaffar Nagar, 1988, p. 74.
15. Prasad, Dr. Rajendra, An Autobiography, Sasta Sahitya Mandal, New Delhi, 1946, p. 456.
16. Congress Resolution on the Kisan Sabha –

   "In view of certain difficulties that has arisen in regard to the Kisan Sabhas and other organisations in some parts of India, the Congress desires to clarify the position and state its attitude towards them. The Congress has already fully recognized the right of the Kisan to organize themselves in peasant unions. Nevertheless it must be remembered that the Congress itself is in the main a Kisan organisation and as its contacts with the masses have increased, numbers of Kisans have joined it and influenced its policy. The Congress must and it has, in fact, stood for these Kisan masses and championed their claims, and has worked for the independence of India which must be based on the freedom from exploitation of all our people. In order to achieve this independence and strengthen the Kisans and realise their demands, it is essential that the Congress be strengthened and that the Kisans should be invited to join it in ever larger numbers and organised to carry on their struggle under its banner. It is the duty of every Congressman to work for the speed of the Congress organization in every village in India and not to do anything which weakens the organization in any way."

"While recognizing the right of the kisans to organize Kisan Sabhas, the Congress cannot associate itself with any activities which are incompatible with the basic principles of the Congress and will not countenance any of the activities of those Congressman who as members of the Kisan Sabhas, help in creating an atmosphere hostile to Congress principles and policy. The Congress, therefore, calls upon provincial Congress committees to bear the above in mind and take suitable action wherever called for." — Tendulkar, D.G., Mahatma, Vol. 4, p. 224.

# CHAPTER VIII

# Conclusion

We have analysed in detail Jawaharlal Nehru's outlook and conduct about the peasantry and its problems in the last seven chapters. We have understood the steps taken by him in future regarding the peasants in which too there was inclusion of the abolition of Zamindari and Taluqdari evilful systems. We have also seen that today how the leaders of peasantry, having measured the circumstances of that period between the peasants and landlords, can prepare an equitable atmosphere between the agriculture labourers and the peasants who are landholders, under the independent and changed environment. It is also vital because even now there are numerous problems being confronted by the peasantry like land reforms – consolidation, cost of production and price, labour and return, price of crops etc. – and simultaneously the condition of agricultural labourer, who works with the peasant in field, is not yet so much reformed (improved) proportionately as it should have been. By the green revolution the agricultural labourers are not so much benefited as they should have been. The peasants have to understand and think over these facts.

Though in the field of production as the peasants have made progress and as they have enhanced the glory of them, society and the country, it is worth to pay hearty thanks to the government and its chief for eighteen years Jawaharlal Nehru, yet the more praise should be done of the struggle done by him and the ideal socialism grown out of it. The seven chapters which have been read, how much significant each one out of them it was at that time the same way it is today. It is important not only for India but for all the countries having the agriculture as main profession throughout the world and especially the developing countries too. Due to his link with the Oudh peasantry, leadership of the Oudh Kisan Sabha, and in the same region (Oudh) through starting the Eka movement he had taken a vow to get sanctioned for the peasants justice and status of equality with the end of their miseries. In this country the custom of rent realization from the peasants was really in the form of serious exploiting system. Mahatma Gandhi while opposing this system in 1918, had given the direction of Satyagraha against the forcible realization of rent to the Kaira district peasants of Gujarat and in Nadiad with the commencement of Satyagraha about rent he said, "In fact the rent is realized from the production which comes in. Forcible rent realization in the absence of production is injustice. But in this country it has become a rule that the peasants are not to be believed irrespective of truth in their statements and they are to be exploited extremely. So, this extremity and this injustice will have to be opposed."[1] Having extended further Gandhiji's this formula Nehru bore the responsibility of ending the evilful rent system and oppression caused by it. While accomplishing it he passed through the struggles of provincial and national level, for – against the policies and party programmes, the extreme – liberal and soft-hot currents but finally while moving ahead step by step he had made the peasants stand at a decisive result. The end of Bhawali system, liberation of the peasants and land to the tiller, implementation of these systems under the leadership of Nehru and his colleagues were not lesser achievements. In a form it was actually socio-economic transformation or transition.

Nehru's ideal socialism came out of his link with the peasantry and his thinking of making an end of their (peasants) miseries. And he aimed at implementing this socialism in its true form just with getting of the independence. To fulfil this aim Nehru remained busy in associating closely the peasantry with the political movement. In this participation of the peasantry while having proved his honesty and seriousness he left out for future the following ways for the leaders of the peasantry and the well-wishers of the peasants :

(a) To pick up from root the problems of peasants and to see these from socio-economic sight and to seek solution of these accordingly, not adopting for these the sight of political interest. For it in the end of 1930, Nehru had clearly said, 'Peasants require to be made prosperous socially and economically, so, the battle should be fought on these fronts.'[2]

(b) While working for the peasantry, one has to become peasant or the standard of living of peasant one has to adopt because the imposed leadership cannot be proved effective among the peasants. Nehru himself had abondoned his super class standard of living and while facing every hardship he went village to village, door to door in the midst of peasantry and thus, he could arouse self confidence, courage of bearing hardship and courage to oppose gallantly in the peasants.

(c) Nehru's inspiration, to get the independence and to get the peasants liberated from miseries, went side by side. This important chapter has been of the period of national liberation movement. Today the peasants can solve rest of the different problems regarding the land and tilling, having moved it ahead. Undoubtedly the country's progress even today depends on the land works. It is essential for it that the discontentment of the peasants should be abated with the country's progress. Today the problems of rent, irrigation charges and consolidation are tantamount to none. It is unique achievement of Nehru in the independent India but even now there is necessity of developing agriculture on the basis of technology and science. Simultaneously having the peasants relieved from the old systems, they require to be taught that they should do the agriculture work like an industry. It is to be given priority in the thinking of peasant leaders.

(d) Nehru's thinking about the peasants contained two levels. Its first level was – getting sanctioned the relief and social equality to the peasants in pre-independence period. For it Nehru also did all that, as it is obvious in the analysis of this book evidently. The second level was of the independence and with it the self reliance of the peasants. In this form the abolition of Zamindari system, land of the tiller and lease-hold to the landless persons were the results of his efforts. Ahead of it towards the

> self reliance of the peasants the work was done – to solve the problem of sub-division and further division in pieces of the land and to enthuse them (the peasants) for cooperative sector, so that in the future they may be rescued from the clutches of moneylenders, parasites and profiteers. Nehru did work for it. The first five year plan (1951-52 to 1955-56) we can quote for it here. In this plan, with irrigation and electricity, agriculture was given priority. For the development of these Rs. 2,378 crores, or 44% of the budget of the whole of plan, were spent."[3]

The cooperative system was a special thing but in spite of the differences of thoughts and line of action, also having faced difficulties Nehru remained busy in making this programme a movement. Today all over the country most of the cooperative societies are working for the loans of agriculture purposes. "In the end of June, 1981, 94019 primary agriculture loan committees were fulfilling the needs of 96 per cent rural areas. By the same time about 6 crore persons were the members of these cooperative societies. It was definitely a special, important and planned step." About twenty years period from 1960-61 to 1980-81, of a big achievement in cooperative sector is given at next page which is the detail description of Nehru's thoughts regarding the development of agriculture and rural areas.

How much prosperous and self-reliant the peasantry would become? It would be the real basis of the country's development and it would be the real meaning of the country's independence. Nehru fundamentally took this concept, otherwise, he would have not made the rent and reduction in it the subject of the peasants struggle. For example we can cite No-rent Movement of 1931-32, of United Provinces. In this movement the abatement of rent was the main demand and according to the statement of government "the total rent recovery from the whole province in 49 districts was Rs. 20,701,735."[5]

And the rent was the main resource of the government's income during British period but today the government of independent India has already forgiven the rent of petty peasants while the rest of the whole rent is being given to villages panchayats so that it (rent) may be utilised in villages by these (panchayats). Not only it but after the independence the peasants were never forced to pay rent as it was being done during the landlord system under the British regime. The reasons are : the step of peasantry towards self-reliance and its social, political and economic freedom. The same was the longing of Nehru. Growth of production, prosperity and self-reliance became major tasks for the peasants and the problem of rent (of paying) became just secondary one for them.

**The Development of Cooperative Societies**

| | 1960-61 | 1970-71 | 1975-76 | 1977-78 | 1978-79 | 1979-80 | 1980-81 |
|---|---|---|---|---|---|---|---|
| No. of cooperative societies in lacs | 3.3 | 3.2 | 3.1 | 3.0 | 3.0 | 2.9 | 3.0 |
| No. of membership in lacs | 342 | 591 | 848 | 931 | 1,014 | 1,010 | 1,062 |
| No. of shares in crores | 222 | 581 | 1,529 | 1,812 | | 1,987 | 2,088 |
| Invested capital in crores | 1,312 | 6,810 | 12,432 | 16,631 | 18,904 | 19,058 | 20,021 |

These above-mentioned were the ideals which in principle and practice he (Nehru) adopted and through planning by the medium of government he gave us too these and he, with the thought of socialism, showed the way of progress to the peasants. Having adopted these ideals, in future the solution of the rest of problems of this class (the peasantry) would be possible.

## The importance of Nehru and the peasantry in their historical and political background of their age and its appraisal :

In their political and historical background the importance of Jawaharlal Nehru and the peasantry is very heavy and easily it cannot be appraised. Especially having seen these following sentences we can imagine the contribution of this class :

(a) In the United Provinces at the provincial level 'if there would have been no leadership of Nehru to the Kisan Sabha in 1920-21, perhaps the Eka peasants movement would not have been fought so efficiently and undauntedly. Nehru had provided that (movement) with the wonderful strength of courage and he had given them the message of courage having reached in middle of the peasants gathering while having crossed even the raised (alerted) bayonets of army in 1921, in Rai Bareli'.[7] It is also clear that if the Eka movement in United Provinces would have been associated with the Congress and Gandhiji's programme as it is also clear from the analysis, in the United Provinces the Non-cooperation and Khilafat movement would have been secondary or not so successful where it was not prior strong and rampant. The peasants struggle had given life to it (the Non-cooperation and Khilafat movement).

(b) This fact is true that after Gandhiji's rise on Indian political field, the common men, rural and peasants, became busy in the struggle for independence. But there was important place of the peasant struggles in the making of becoming busy of common men and while giving its credit Jawaharlal Nehru and the United Provinces cannot be minimized in their appraisal. The peasants struggle of United Provinces was most organised movement in the history of all the peasant struggles of India."[8] It had shown the way for the whole of India. In comparison also of that age's Kerala's Malabar's peasants rebellion against the Namboodri landlords, this struggle of the peasants of United Provinces, fought under the leadership of Jawaharlal Nehru and his colleagues, was very weighty, influential and important. It is historical fact.

(c) In the background of that age's occurrences if we see these seriously, we find that the strength which was shown by Oudh peasants in 1920-21, 'that got duly sanctioned the right of permanent tenancy on land for the peasants in 1929'.[10] Though at the time of struggle in 1921, 'The Revenue Secretary of United Provinces in his report, to the government of India, had expressed necessity that in the interest of peasants the step would have to be taken.'[11] But the government had passed eight years in favour of landlords and before facing the next peasants movement in 1929, made the Act. The same way in 1931-32, the No-rent Movement of United Provinces had itself gained strength while having inflicted heavy blow on the landlord system and it had taken step towards demolishing this system once and for all. Simultaneously it had forced the government for the first time to appoint such committee which could think over the realization of rent on the basis of consideration of the crop's price and its cost of production'.[12] It could be done due to the growing strength and awakening of peasants, and in this committee fearfully could have entered the representatives of landowners and landlords; otherwise such demands were not allowed to be heard even by the landlords and the government. Subsequently the strength of peasants developed all over the country and Nehru having got himself associated on the national level with it, gave direction to the peasants and their organisations. It resulted in the day-by-day lightening of burden from the peasant's shoulders and their (the peasants) development in the form of a respectable social class hastily.

Finally to take the peasants in the present state (condition) and to make them self-reliant in every sphere, there has been the major contribution of Nehru. Not only this but to turn the peasants towards the independence struggle, there has been his important role. The leadership which was provided by him to the peasants and which yielded the socialist ideals for the future of peasantry, the importance of these will be growing in every time to come in context whether there is question of solving the problems of peasants or to organise them or to take them more firmly in the stream of national development or to eradicate their miseries.

## References

1. Kumar, Dr. Ravindra, Social and Political Ideas of Sardar Vallabhbhai J. Patel, p. 95 (Original-Home Political 1918, F. No. 3/18, National Archives of India, New Delhi).
2. Home Department Political 1930, F. No. 12/30, National Archives of India, New Delhi.
3. India 1980 (Yearly Journal of Ministry of Information and Broadcasting, Government of India), p. 274.

4. India 1983, p. 371.
5. Home Political 1931, F. No. 33/16 and K.W. National Archives of India, New Delhi.
6. India 1983, p. 371.
7. Nehru, Pandit Jawahar Lal, An Autobiography (sixth edition), 1988, p. 314.
8. Namboodiripad, E.M.S., A History of Indian Freedom Struggle, Social Scientist Press, Trivandrum, 1986, p. 470.
9. *Ibid.*
10. Home Department Political 1930, F. No. 10/2/30, National Archives of India, New Delhi.
11. Home Department Political 1921, F. No. 13/21, National Archives of India, New Delhi.
12. Home Department Political 1931, F. No. 33/31, National Archives of India, New Delhi.

# Appendices

## Appendix 1

**Home Department Political 1920**
**File No. 6/1920**
**National Archives of India, New Delhi**

"Much of the speech-making and violent decaration are campaigning tactics to catch votes at the next elections. The Kisan Sabha is being similarly worked. An indication of the propaganda going on among tenants is shown by an incident that happened lately in Pratapgarh. An agitator there induced a couple of hundred of the tenants to march into Allahabad to see Mr. Gandhi and represent to him their grievances against Zamindars. The organization of the Kisan Sabha in Allahabad got hold of the tenants and held meetings and have been actively interesting themselves in supporting them. Two of the leaders went off to Pratapgarh to make enquiries into the alleged severities and to urge the people to form Kisan Sabhas and to formulate their demands and grievances collectively. A private meeting of Taluqdars and Zamindars was held at Pratapgarh to consider their position. Meetings of Kisan Sabhas are also reported from Farukhabad, where there were big attendances, and the new council elections were fully discussed."

# Appendix 2

## Agrarian Disturbances in Rae Bareli

By a special correspondent of 'The Leader'.

"Since I wired to you last things have been going on very badly with the poor, oppressed, misguided kisans. When I wrote to you on the 11th instant that there were no disturbances any longer, it seems I should have added, 'except trouble created by men to whom we look up as the guardians of law and order and the representatives of the ancient traditions of our Indian society.' I have seen a large number of kisans from different villages. Their tale of sufferings is woeful. Some of them have been brutally beaten by policemen without the knowledge of or permission of the Superintendent of Police. Certain taluqdars have taken the law into their own hands. The police have arrested about 400 persons. The servants of some taluqdars also have placed some kisans under their own custody. It is felt that the Governor's telegram of congratulations was very ill-advised. Even then it is not too late to mend matters. Pandit Madan Mohan Malviya and Pandit Venkatesh Narain Tewary have arrived here and are doing their little bit to relieve the distress of the poor kisans. But non-officials cannot stop the oppression that is going on."

*Young India*, Ahmedabad
January 26, 1921
Edited by M.K. Gandhi.

## Appendix 3

### The Peasant Movement and the Progress of Non-Co-operation in the United Provinces

Young India, Ahmedabad,
August 11, 1921.
Edited by Mahatma Gandhi.

"Swaraj Fund Rs. 4,10,737, Congress Membership 3,28,966, Spinning wheels 2,81,525, Suspensions of legal practice 113, Panchayats 3000, Surrender of honours (Chow magistracies, durbaridams, war medals, village headmasterships) 10. National school 126, students 10,500. Resignations of Professors and teachers 76."

## Appendix 4

**'Statement of Jawaharlal Nehru'**
**17 January, 1930**

*'Economic Ruin of Indian Peasants by Britishers'*

"India has been economically. The revenue derived from our people is out of all proportion to our income. Our average income is 7 pice (less than two pence) per day and of the heavy taxes we pay. 20 per cent are raised from the peasantry and 3 per cent from the salt tax which falls most heavily on the poor. Village industries such as hand spinning have been destroyed leaving peasantry for at least four months in the year and dulling their intellect for want of handicrafts and nothing has been substituted as in other countries for the craft thus destroyed."

– Jawaharl Lal Nehru,
*The Hindustan Times*, page 1,
20 January, 1930.

# Appendix 5

## Speech of Jawaharlal Nehru in a Kisan meeting at Kotharaj, Distt. Allahabad on 20-6-31

"Kisan Brethren,

At the outset I have to beg your pardon for arriving very late here. I have come here just after attending another big meeting at Sulahpore. Then there are more than one meetings to attend, it is difficult to attend all in time."

"I have got many things to tell you, but will not probably be able to do so at this time. You are in a hurry and I too cannot remain very long here. I have been out of province for two months and have just returned to Allahabad after a very long journey. For many days I remained at Ceylon, so I am not very well acquainted with the condition of the province for the past one or two months. Since my return here I have been hearing how repression and injustices are being committed against the Kisans of our district and of others in the province; how they are forced to pay their rent, beaten with lathi and prosecuted; and that Sec. 107 has been used against many workers."

"Hearing this I was much pained and troubled and also pained me much to learn that you are entangled in the calamity in this way. I had agreed to attend two or three of your Sabhas to have a talk with you and to give you some advice, but the fact is that before doing so I wish to consult a few Congress workers present here and Mahatma Gandhi the Congress Empire. At present it is a bit difficult for one man to advise you with much responsibility. You know we have launched a great struggle for complete Swaraj in which many Hindus, Mohammadons and Kisans helped us, as they rightly knew that it would be beneficial to them and their grievances would thereby be removed. They offered help merely because they knew that Swaraj means removal of their difficulties and poverty of masses. Who are the masses of India? They are not a few citizens or Vakils but are really kisan of the villages. When the difficulties of Kisans are not removed, of what avail the swaraj would be? Swaraj really means the removal of difficulties of the masses of India specially kisans regarding theiur rent, ejectment, possession over their land, etc. Such swaraj would really be of no avail to them. Therefore Swaraj mean that there would be no foreign Government in the country and no individual in the capacity of a Raja or Maharaja or Governor should be its ruler. Our swaraj means a Panchayati Raj in the country in which there will be no distinction between the ruler and the ruled and we wish that all the ruled should become the ruler of the country. There should be a Panchayat in the country of all its people which might manage its affairs. The Panches who are temporarily your Raja should be your servant as well. There are two forms of government : one by force, lathi, gun and jail, with the strength of army, police, lathi and gun behind it and if the people refuse to obey its order it would make them to obey by being force, and gun and by terrifying them vith strength of army and jail; the other form of government is that in which people in consultation with one another establish Panchayati Raj without any use of force or any body. Under this Government there would be very little need for lathi, gun, army and the Police. Now-a-days there exist a govt. of lathi, gun and army in the country and whatever is done is not done with your consultation. One officer passes order for you to obey and if you do not approve of it, it will be enforced on you through police and army without your consent. What sort of Govt. we want? We want such a Govt. under which all, with mutual consultation after establishing a Panchayati Raj, manage the affairs. No Panch can use lathi or gun for his work and if he does so he will be removed. Therefore there are two forms of Govt. one which we are in our country under which cases are instituted and ejectments are enforced in this way, people are sent to jail and efforts are made to realize rent, and the other Govt. is of Panchayat and we hope that it will soon be established in the country when there will be swaraj in it. Kisans have joined the little for swaraj with a view to establish Panchayati Raj and have their grievances removed through it otherwise there was no necessity for them to have swaraj under which their condition and their troubles regarding rent remain continue as they are now. This sort of swaraj would be of no good to them and that they do not require it. For this very swaraj the country and the Congress have not launched the battle. Mahatmaji, you know is a big leader, but he is so because we have appointed him as such and none else has placed him on us, like such as Governor etc. of the present day who are appointed from our own selection. Who appointed Mahatmaji? The people of the country who had love for him and entertained confidence in him and appointed him as their leader or officer. Suppose, tomorrow you don't keep confidence in him you can remove him and appoint another man instead. We like him so we keep him. You should remember that as we have appointed him he had got our strength behind him. Take for example the case of the Governor; what strength he has got behind him? He has got the strength of gun and sword behind him through which he can commit oppressions and can take work from you by putting you in fear. We have launched the battle for swaraj under the lead of Mahatmaji and you, not only you, but the people of the whole country participated in it because of their love for it. They were tired of their troubles and how they fought the battle and how thousands of our brethren went to jail for it. Both the Hindus and Musalmans took part in it with the result that the British Govt. became perplexed. The British Govt. is a strong Govt. and not a weak one. It knows how to fight a big battle but they too had to acknowledge the bravery of those who are fighting the Congress battle. The Govt. and the English nation cannot check thousands of people and crores of kisans who are fighting the battle for swaraj. Can police check them when they are prepared to suffer lathi blows? The result of the battle had been that the name of the country excelled in bravery throughout the world, which after all came to know that Indians are very brave. Formerly the world knew that Indians who are ruled by a handful of men are slaves and 33 crores of Hindus and Muslims of the place bow down their heads and receive kicks like slaves. Everybody commits oppressions on them whatever he likes. The people of the countries Germany, America, Japan and also the people of England the country of the English knew that Indians are slaves but the last years struggle has lead them to think that they are brave who can fight for the freedom and swaraj and can make sacrifice for it and that their country is about to become free it has fought the battle bravely. We have produced great effect on the British Government and the nation with the result that they desired to have a compromise with us. You know that there was some talk between Mahatma Gandhi and the Viceroy some two months ago as a result of which we promised to suspend the struggle for some time to have a talk on the compromise. If a compromise is arrived at resulting in swaraj under which all grievances of kisans are removed so much so good and we are glad to accept it. But what sort of compromise is it which does not result in swaraj. When terms were offered on the side of British, Mahatmaji agreed to them and suspended the battle from his side. On the side of the British, you know, many prisoners were released from jail, how ordinances were cancelled. The gave permission to manufacture salt for which we first started our battle that is they permitted kisans to manufacture salt in villages if they so like. They accepted all these things. They were told that we are entitled to picket the foreign cloth and will do it. It was made quite clear at the time of the truce that we shall barish foreign cloth from the country and forbid the sale of liquor. We are entitled to picket these things and shall continue to make efforts so long as the foreign cloth is in the country whether there is a truce or not. From our side it was also said that during the period of the truce we shall not have recourse to satyagraha, defy laws, and launch no-tax campaign for the sake of struggle. All these things were settled. Three months have since elapsed but no talk for any compromise has commenced. It is not yet known where the conference will take place, either in India or in England and it is also a matter under consideration whether anybody on behalf of the Congress should go there or not, suppose, if we think that we are being divided and are called there for that very purpose we used not go there then, and if we think that honest and sincere talk for compromise would take place thereon represent alive of the congress either Mahatma Gandhi or anybody else whom the country and the kisans would like to go there as we are not to send crows there. When we shall start struggle all will participate in it but at this time one man is quite sufficient for there. No talk for compromise has begun yet; it is only in name so far, but what is being done against kisans, how excesses are being committed to realise rent, how they are pressed, cases are instituted against them. It is a matter of great regret that at one or two places highhandedness has also been practice in the aids of the kisans but wherever such incidents have occurred, the kisans of the places becoming tired of the atrocities and oppressions have committed such mistakes, which is a matter of great regret indeed and I hope that they would adopt to the principle that they would not raise their hands and have recourse to satyagraha if they were to start satyagraha battle they might have done so after mutual consultation. When once a thing has been decided and they have accepted the advice of Mahatma Gandhi to fight the battle peacefully, they ought to have remembered it. The breach of the peace has resulted in great loss to the kisans and not in any good to them. You have to fight battles and have to do other big things still; the important question of swaraj is before us and we have also taken the question of kisans in hand. You are quite aware that your forefathers had undergone great calamities and you too are being ejected from your lands. All these questions will have to be taken in hand with a view to remove your grievances which cannot be removed without pains and for which we shall have to make efforts. Remember if you adopt the path of violence, it would in no way benefit you. We wish to adopt methods through which we have already shown to the whole world last year how brave our country is. It is the first thing which you are to keep in mind."

"The second thing is, that on one side talks for compromise are in progress and on the other atrocities are being committed on kisans. Congress workers are arrested and securities under section 107 are demanded from them. Section 144 are promulgatod and every other thing is going on. It is not a talk for compromise at all when the truce was going on we clearly said that we prepared to advise kisans to suspend no-tax campaign and after that we informed the Viceroy of the condition of kisans and their plight owing to cheapness. We also said that do not understand that as the truce has been effected we can ask the kisans to pay their full rent. They cannot pay it in full and so the zamindars their revenue. We shall of course ask them to pay as much as they can but we at the same time know that they are unable to pay the full. We will request you to remit the major portion of the rent and then only can the compromise be effected as it is quite impossible for the kisans to pay their full rent. This fact was also admitted by them as they knew that the conditions of kisans are bad. We accepted the truce on this very condition and we made it quite clear to them that the kisans cannot pay the full rent. They would pay as much as they easily can and whatever would be decided by mutual consultation would be paid. We are certainly anxious for a compromise as we do not want to create any trouble. We want that kisans might not be put to any trouble for which we have tried much and are still trying for the same. Mahatmaji after travelling hundreds of miles visited our province with a view to think over as to what can be done for the kisans and zamindars. He had a talk with the Governor and issued a pamphlet which you migh have seen. He tried his level best for the kisans and zamindars both as he does not want a struggle between the both. He went one place for ward from what the Congress decided in the case of kisans and after giving a thorough thinking to the matter has decided to go one place forward in the question. He would ask those who have got occupancy rights to pay upto -/12/- and thus -/4/- would be remitted to them and those who are non-occupancy tenants -/8/- should be remitted to them. Those who pay -/12/- or -/8/- should have a receipt for the full amount. Suppose one man has already paid -/8/- and still a decree is passed against him for the arrear (the remitted sum) followed by his ejectment, he will be nowhere then. Therefore whatever will be paid will be done after having a receipt for full. Suppose -/8/- have been decided to be paid and an individual is not in a position to pay in full; the zamindar then can write in the receipt that -/8/- have been remitted and a receipt for -/4/- which have been received in part payment is issued. All should be made quite clear. Some zamindars have accepted it but most of them have not done so which can not be helped. We have tried to settle things amicably but they (zamindars) are not agreeing to that. We again ask you to pay whatever you easily can and if you can pay whatever Mahatmaji has advised you, you must pay and if nobody agrees to have it, it cannot be helped. We ask you and zamindars both to settle the matter amicably with love and thus help each other. But the question for the present is about the realization. Efforts are being made to realise rent from you by force and by filing cases. It is a separate question. I tell you to pay whatever you can but at the same time I also say that you should not pay a single pice to anybody by lathi force. We were ready to pay what we could but it was not accepted then and now it is realized by lathi force, by instituted cases effecting ejectments. It is degrading to pay in this manner and I would tell you to ask your zamindar to have a compromise with you saying them that we are ready to pay but if you realise it by the force of lathi we shall not pay a single sheell to you. We are not so degraded and like beasts that you are to put as to humiliation in this way. No gentleman would like to pay a pice in this manner, but if you have compromise with us we shall pay you whatever we can. We fought so much for swaraj, underwent sufferings, went to jail and suffered lathi blows, what all this fair? Only for the sake of getting our grievances removed. If you are perplexed at this time out of fear of lathi and ejectment and thus weaken yourself and if your zamindars realizing it comes to know that it is an easy thing to keep you under control and a consequence arrest you like sheep to bring cases against you, your sacrifices then are of no avail. We are to sit at ease only when we get our rights. Kisans get their rights. Today there is a question of remission of rent as to what should be paid and what not but the main question before you and the country is regarding the full remission of rent. The principle of the Congress in this concern is to secure permanent remission of rent and revenue and that can only be had when we have strength in our hands. For the present we are fighting for the swaraj with a view to strengthen the hands of masses of India which do not constitute the Congress, Mahatmaji or any other individual, but it constitutes all the people of the country. Therefore we are fighting for swaraj to strengthen the hands of the masses so that we may be able to frame laws than for the removal for the grievances of kisans and make permanent reduction in their rent. If I am asked I can say that my principle is quite clearly against this zamindar class. I think that everybody should be the owner of his land. I cannot agree to any other principle. This will have to be decided by the country. It is a matter of great pleasure if my opinion is accepted, I have let you know my views. But there is another question before you, that is, what you should do under the circumstances when you are pressed and rent is realised by force? Regarding this I must tell you that you should say clearly that you are prepared to pay what Mahatmaji has asked you to do, but are not ready to do so by force of lathi; the more you will be oppressed the greater you will get strength. You should tell them that by committing atrocities, holding threats and by beating you cannot be ruled over nor rent can be realized. If anybody brings you to the right path it can only be with your own pleasure."

"I must tell you this that you should not be perplexed and if you become nervous at this juncture it will mean that the sacrifices you made last year and are now making are all wasted. If a compromise is effected, we wish it may be, and swaraj be achieved, so much so good because if our object is gained by peaceful means it is no good to engage in fight for it and if no compromise is arrived at we shall have to accept the same ways, take to satyagraha, suffer lathi blows and do such other things for which we should hold overselves in readiness. A country which keeps itself in readiness can fight out a battle and can bring about a compromise as well which is always effected with the strong. Therefore you shall have to hold yourself in readiness. You are to strengthen the organization of the Congress and the kisans and remove the foreign cloth and liquor from the country. Remember if we are perplexed owing to pressure and fear and prove that kisans become nervous by lathi blows, situation of cases and that they have no strength; it will purely lead to their ejectments and then if they complain of it and of passing decrees against them, he has nothing to say about it. We have got no authority of court and no strength or army through which we can be able to stop ejectments. This we cannot do, nor we can help you if you are ejected or subjected to other oppressions. We can help you in one way that is we can continue the struggle vigorously resulting in swaraj, then only we see who have been ejected and who have been oppressed. We can then restore theirs land to them and help them in other ways. This can be had only when we have got powers in our hands, therefore we can do nothing at this time but to make efforts for the acheivement of swaraj."

One thing more you would remember at this time that none should have the ejected lands and thus should help one another, otherwise it is nothing but to cut ones throat. You should co-operate with others to so that you get strengthened and if there are ill-feelings among you you can easily be crushed. Therefore you should not become nervous at the existing atrocities but at the same time I tell you that we are unable to help you and so we cannot give you any promise for the same. You have to fight again and the method of our struggle are quite different. When time comes we shall fight, how recourse to satyagraha, defy laws and do all other things but whatever we have to do, would do like an army or a sepoy that is we shall do it with a united force. A handful of men should not start a struggle at this time. Keep your self in readiness and when the struggle for no-tax campaign is launched we shall face it (struggle) with all strength. At this time pay what you can and if it is realised by lathi force, tell them clearly that not a single pice will be paid. In conclusion you should bear in mind that none should have the ejected land."

*Prepared by :*

Parshottam Das,
Inspector C.I.D. (2.7.1931)
P. Archives, U.P., Lucknow, 7/31.

# Appendix 6

## Extracts of the Presidential Address, Indian National Congress, Forty-ninth Session April 1936, Lucknow

Allahabad Law Journal Press,
Allahabad.

"I am convinced that the only way to the solution of the world's problems and of India's problems lies in socialism and when I use this word I do so not in a vague humanitarian way, but in the scientific economic sense. Socialism, however, is even more than an economic doctrine, it is a philosophy of life and as such it appeals to me. I see no way of ending the poverty, the vast unemployment, the degradation and the subjection of the Indian people, except through socialism, that involves vast and revolutionary changes, the ending of vested interests in land and industry as well as the feudal and autocratic Indian state system, that means the ending of Private property except in a restricted sense and the replacement of the present profit system by a higher ideal of co-operative service. It means ultimately a change in our instincts and habits. In short it means a new civilization radically different from the present capitalist order. Some glimpse, we can have of this new civilization in the Territories of U.S.S.R. Much has happened there which has pained me greatly and with which I disagree, but I look upon that great and fascinating unfolding of a new order and a new civilization as the most promising feature of our dismalage."

"Socialism is thus for me not merely an economic doctrine which I favour; it is a vital creed which I hold with all my head and heart. I work for India's independence because the nationalist in me cannot tolerate alien domination. I work for it even more because for me it is the inevitable step to the social and economic changes. I should like the Congress to become a socialist organization and to join hands with the other forces in the world who are working for the new civilization."

"Much as I insist for the achievement of socialism in this country. I have no desire to force the issue in the Congress and thereby create difficulties in the way of our struggle for independence. I shall co-operate greatly and with all the strength in me with all those who work for independence even though they do not agree with the socialist solution. But I shall do so stating my position frankly and hoping to convert the Congress and the country to it, for it is only thus can I see it achieving independence.

# Appendix 7

## "Congress Resolution on the Agrarian Programme"

"The Congress is of opinion that the most important and urgent problem of the country is the appalling poverty, unemployment and indebtedness of the peasantry which is fundamentally due to the antiquated and repressive land tenure and revenue systems and intensified in recent years by the great slump in prices of the agricultural produce."

"The final solution of this problem inevitably involves the removal of British imperialistic exploitation, through change of the land tenure and revenue systems and recognition by the state of its duty to provide work for the rural and unemployed masses. In view, however, of the fact that agrarian conditions and land tenure and revenue system differ in the various provinces, it is desirable to consult the provincial Congress committees and also such peasants' organizations as the working committee thinks fit in the drawing up of a full all-India agrarian programme, as well as the programme for each province."

"This Congress, therefore, calls upon each provincial Congress committee to make recommendations in detail to the working committee by August 1, 1936, for being considered and placed before the All India Congress Committee, having particular regard to following matters :

1. Freedom of organisation of agricultural labourers and peasants;
2. Safeguarding the interests of peasants where there are intermediaries between the state and themselves;
3. Just and fair relief of agricultural indebtedness, including arrears of rent and revenue;
4. Emancipation of peasants from feudal and semi-feudal levies;
5. Substantial reduction in respect of rent and revenue demands;

6. A just allotment of the state expenditure for social, economic and cultural amenities of the villages;
7. Protection against harassing restrictions on the utilisation of local natural facilities for their domestic and agricultural needs;
8. Freedom from oppression and harassment at the hand of Government officials and landlords; and
9. Fostering of industries for relieving rural unemployment."

D. No. 4/8/36
Home Deptt. Political 1936,
National Archives of India,
New Delhi.

# Bibliography

**(A)**


Antonova, K.A., Bogard Levin, G.M. and Kotivaski, G.G; History of India, Progress Publications, Moscow, U.S.S.R. First (Hindi) edition 1984.

Chandra Tara, History of India (Part 1 to 3), Publication Division, New Delhi; First (Hindi) edition, 1982.

Desai, Mahadeo Harilal, The Story of Bardoli, Navjeevan Publishing House, Ahmedabad, Second Edition.

Guha, A.C.; India's Struggle Quarter of a Century, Publication Division, New Delhi, First edition, 1982.

Kumar, Ravindra, Contribution of Maulana Abul Kalama Azad in solution of the Problem of Communalism and National Liberation Movement in India, Rajeev Prakashan Mandir, Muzaffarnagar, First (Hindi), edition 1989.

Kumar, Ravindra; Life and Work of Kanjibhai Desai, Suruchi Trust Surat, First (Hindi) edition, 1989.

Kumar, Ravindra; Pandit Jawaharlal Nehru and the Peasants Movement, Atlantic Publishers and Distributors, New Delhi, First edition 1990.

Kumar, Ravindra; Sardar Vallabhbhai Patel and Com. Mao Tse-Tung: A Comparative Study, Rajeev Prakashan Mandir, Muzaffarnagar, First (Hindi) edition, 1988.

Kumar, Ravindra; Social and Political Ideas of Sardar Vallabhbhai J. Patel, Mittal Publications, New Delhi, First (Hindi) edition, 1991.

Majoomdar, R.C.; History of Freedom Movement in India, Calcutta, 1962.

Namboodiripad, E.M.S; A History of Indian Freedom Struggle, Social Scientist Press, Trivandrum, First edition, 1986.

Nehru, Jawaharlal; An Autobiography, Jawaharlal Nehru Memorial Fund, New Delhi, Sixth edition, 1988.

Nehru, Jawaharlal, President's Speech, 49th Session of Indian National Congress, April 1936 (Lucknow), Allahabad Law Journal Press, Allahabad, First edition, 1936.

Parikh, Narhari Dwarkadas and Shah Uttam Chand Deep Chand, Speeches of Sardar Vallabhbhai Patel, Navjeevan Publishing House, Ahmedabad, First (Hindi) edition, 1949.

Prasad, Rajendar, An Autobiography, Sasta Sahitya Mandal, New Delhi, Third (Hindi) edition, 1962.

Rao, V.K.R.V.; The Nehru Legacy, New Delhi, First edition, 1970.

Sangwan, Surajmal; Peasants Struggle and Mutinies in Indian History, A.P. Press, New Delhi, First (Hindi), edition, 1984.

Tendulkar, D.G.; 'Mahatma' (1 to 6), Publication Division, New Delhi-19

## (B)

Original Documents used from Home Department (Political), National Archives of India, New Delhi.

*Year 1920* (Deposit)

File No. 6/20 (B)

File No. 7/20 (B)

*Year 1921*

File No. 7/21

File No. 13/21 (B)

File No. 13/21

File No. 2/13/21

File No. 10/21

*Year 1930*

File No. 10(x)/257/30

File No. 257/30

File No. 33/11 and K.W.

File No. 4/8 (No. S.D. 9205)/30
File No. 32 and K.W.
File No. 25/30
File No. 10/30
File No. 11/30
File No. 12/30

*Year 1931*

File No. 1/31
File No. 3/31
File No. 23/33/31
File No. 24/2/31
File No. 27/3/31
File No. 31/31
File No. 32/31
File No. 33(I)/31
File No. 33(II)/31
File No. 33/10/31
File No. 33/XI/31
File No. 33/X/31 and K.W.
File No. 33/24/31
File No. 33/27/31
File No. 34/31/31
File No. 46/31
File No. 47/31
File No. 247/31

*Year 1933*

File No. 13/16/33 and K.W.
File No. 33/24/33

*Year 1936*

File No. 4/7/36
File No. 4/8/36
File No. 14/13/36
File No. 37/3/36
File No. 38/4/36
File No. 39/4/36

**(C)**

Original Documents used from the Provicial Archives of Uttar Pradesh, Lucknow.

*Year 1930-31*

File No. 17/2/30 I

File No. 27/3/31

File No. 37/10/31

**(D)**

**Newspapers/Periodicals**

1. (a) India, 1980, Yearly book of the Government of India, Published by the Publication Division, New Delhi.

   (b) India, 1983.

2. The Hindustan Times, New Delhi, January 20, 1930.

3. Young India, Edited by Mahatma Gandhi from Navjeevan Press, Ahmedabad,

   (a) January 26, 1921.

   (b) January 27, 1921.

# Index

## I



## J



## K



## L



## M

## N



## O



## P



## Q



## R

## S



## T



## U



## V



## W



## Y



## Z